Guidelines for Communication

Guidelines for Communication

The Right Tool for Preparing Great Speeches

Fourth Edition, Revised and Expanded

for students, public speakers, and all communicators

Written by Mark Singer
Illustrated by Pegge Patten

1841 Moulton Avenue

North Muskegon, Michigan 49445

877-907-8646

First Edition published 1989
Second Edition 1999
Third Edition 2002
Fourth Edition 2006
Printed in the United States of America

Color House Graphics
3505 Eastern Avenue SE
Grand Rapids, Michigan 49508

Singer, Mark and Patten, Pegge
Guidelines for Communication: The Right Tool for Preparing Great Speeches

Illustrated by Pegge Patten
Designed by Tracey L. Gebbia
Edited by Nancy Taylor

Special thanks to Dr. Vincent L. Lombardi, professor at Michigan State University, for his inspiration throughout the years.

ISBN-10: 0-9707373-5-1
ISBN-13: 978-0-9707373-5-9

Table of Contents

About the Author and Illustrator

Mark Singer, M.A., is a professor of speech communication as well as a radio and television announcer. He holds a Master's degree in communication from Michigan State University. His background includes more than a decade of broadcasting experience and over twenty-five years of college and university teaching. His *Communication Guide,* the core of this book, is a unique blend of his excellent speaking skills and advanced academic training. Singer's primary aim with this work is to have students gain an indispensable tool for creating great speeches.

Pegge Patten, A.A.S., has more than thirty years' experience as a multimedia fine artist. She has studied at the prestigious Academy of Art College in San Francisco and holds a degree in computer graphics and illustration. For this book, Patten has created a series of specially designed, hand-sketched cartoon characters that both inform and entertain. Her artistic contribution makes *Guidelines* a reader-friendly text — students are warmly invited to use their own handwriting to complete the blank sections of the Communication Guides provided within the book.

Introduction

In general, books on speech communication are mostly about theory or mostly about practice. *Guidelines for Communication* is different — it is a *creative blend of both.*

On the practical side, by using this book, students will learn a simple method of how to prepare for any speech by using the very effective Communication Guide. Its use is presented in a step-by-step method so students can complete the blank sections after they read and absorb each chapter. And, if students have any speech anxiety or stage fright, *Guidelines* has more tips than any other book in the field. For students who are preparing for employment interviews, there is a chapter that includes techniques for creating a successful interviewing strategy, sample answers to those "tough questions" from interviewers, tips on proper dress, and specific ideas on how to successfully negotiate for salary and benefits.

On the theoretical side, as students complete the Communication Guide, they will learn the latest and most relevant concepts of communication. For example, on the subject of source credibility, students will learn the theoretical basis for what researchers have found to be the *single most persuasive element in communication.* Other theoretical topics include discussion of the view of communication as *communicare* (Latin for *sharing*), an analysis of the choice of the best ethical standards of communication, and a discussion of the key elements of dyadic communication, such as the norm of reciprocity, turn-taking, topic management, and microgestures.

In a nutshell, by using *Guidelines for Communication,* students of speech communication, and anyone else who requires help and support preparing and delivering speeches, will gain *the right tool for creating great speeches!*

Chapter 1
Communicating for Personal Growth

Communication As Sharing

What is *communication,* and what does it really mean?

The word is derived from the Latin root word *communis* that means "to make common."

And, it is communis that is the source of the Latin word for communicate, namely, *communicare*, which, when translated into English, means "to share."

Therefore, the act of communicating or communication is a kind of sharing, but exactly what kind?

Consider the other words that come from communis: "community," in which people share a land area; "communism," in which people share ownership of property within a society; and "communion," in which people share a relationship with a Higher Power or God. In this light, communication, as it applies to personal relationships, is "the *sharing* of knowledge, attitudes, and behaviors."

Venn diagrams provide a simple way to visualize this. In the first diagram, one circle represents all the information you know, and the other circle represents all the information the other person knows. As you can see, these two circles are separate; this shows that there is no sharing between you and the other person. Hence, in this case, there is no communication. At the point that you and the other person use one or more of the five senses to transfer information, then sharing or communication occurs. And, the more responses that are given to each other's messages, the more communication that is generated. This is what is shown in the second Venn diagram. In this case, as you can see as the blackened area, the same two circles now overlap, showing the amount of communication that has occurred.

Boundaries

Freedom of speech is often compared to waving the arms around the body. We can wave our arms any way that we want with just one boundary — the other person's nose. In other words, in terms of speechmaking, you can communicate anything you want as long as it will not hurt someone's nose, not just physically but also psychologically.

Of course, you can easily see where your arm would *physically* strike another person's nose just by looking. But, have you thought about what types of communication would hit another person's nose in a *psychological* sense?

Here is a list of both types which may be communicated using words or behaviors.

❯ Put-Down: Stating Disrespect for a Person or Her Idea

You're wrong, That's stupid, You stink, That's silly, You're crazy.

❯ Name-Calling: Referring to a Person Using a Negative Label

You're an idiot, You're a [racial or ethnic slur], You're a jerk, You're a bigot.

❯ Threat: Implication of a Future Harm or Punishment

I'll get even with you, just wait until later, The next time you say or do that, I'm going to hurt you by . . . .

❯ Obscenity: A Morally Offensive Message

Any message that is considered as highly insulting to a person's ethics.

As a general rule, *When in doubt, leave it out!* In other words, in planning a speech, a speaker should not risk communicating anything that could be considered obscene.

Nevertheless, for some speeches, such as those containing sexual or violent information, the total exclusion of obscene messages may not be possible. With these speeches, as a way of not offending the audience, a speaker may state a *disclaimer.*

A disclaimer is composed of two or three sentences that: (1) tell the audience the potentially obscene portion of the speech and (2) advise the audience as to how to avoid these potentially offensive messages. A disclaimer is stated either before the speech begins or before the possibly offensive material. The types of choices that an audience member may be offered include closing her eyes, turning her head, putting her hands over her ears, or leaving the room. After the disclaimer, the speaker pauses at least five seconds, which gives audience members enough time to make their choices.

For example, for a presentation about the AIDS virus, a disclaimer before the speech may be, *I will be showing slides from our local hospital of the sexual organs of men and women who are in the advanced stages of AIDS. If you do not wish to see these pictures, could you please leave the room before my speech begins?* The speaker then waits five seconds.

❯ Interference: Creating an Obstacle

Any message that prevents someone from speaking or listening.

This may include sounds such as giggling or laughing, making a face or gesture, and ordinary talking — when these inhibit a person from communicating. Overt actions such as pushing and hitting another person would fall under the type called *physical* interference.

≫ Mean Shouting: Yelling

Any loud volume or high tone of voice expressing anger or rage at another person.

≫ Mean Joking: Humor That Hurts a Person

Any type of entertainment or joke that results in harm to another person.

For example, a speaker cannot remember where she found the statistics in her speech. During the discussion after her speech, one of the audience members responds by saying, *You're a genius when it comes to remembering numbers.* On the surface, this might seem to be a compliment to the speaker. But the comment is actually a form of *sarcasm,* a kind of joke that uses irony to hurt another person. Because the speaker was not prepared, the real meaning of this comment is *You're an idiot* — which is obviously hurtful for the speaker. Nevertheless, members of her audience who notice this double meaning probably consider this remark as only a funny little joke.

How much harm can a simple sarcastic joke like this cause? The word sarcasm comes from the Greek word that means "to tear flesh." So, even though only words were used, the level of hurt may be quite large.

Every one of these types of harm also falls under the category of *criticism* which means "to find fault"; they focus on something wrong, not right, about another person. As such, they definitely are a kind of attack against a person or her ideas, which also is like hitting a person's nose.

Moreover, a highly negative consequence occurs if you use criticism: It is the single most effective way to lower *your* esteem by other people. If you have any doubt, conduct this experiment. Take this book with you, and the next time your supervisor gives you instructions or your teacher asks your opinion, state a put-down, call her a name, and maybe even use a little profanity. After that, how long do you think you will last on your job or continue to be esteemed by your instructor? As far as personal relationships go, if you want to destroy one, nothing is more effective than these criticisms.

So unless destroying all your relationships is your goal, how can you avoid using these criticisms?

Starting with eliminating their use, the next thing to do is to always make "I-statements" and only talk about yourself and your feelings. For example, instead of saying, *You don't know what you're talking about,* make an I-statement by substituting "I" for the subject "You." As a result, the original sentence would become: *I don't know (or understand) what you're talking about.* To an intended receiver, this new version would not be taken as a form of criticism. So, to avoid criticizing anyone, change the subject of your sentences from the other person to yourself — make I-statements whenever you can.

Criticism and Self-Talk

What about how you talk to yourself? Is it okay to criticize yourself as part of your own "self-talk"? In other words, should you choose to talk to yourself in ways that you would not talk to other people?

Based on what you just learned about criticizing others and how damaging that it is, eliminating your highly negative self-talk or extreme self-criticism would seem to be a reasonable goal. As a result of adopting this goal, you can begin to communicate to yourself in ways that increase — not decrease — your self-esteem. Behavioral researchers such as Dr. Shad Helmstetter have found that this combination, eliminating negative self-talk and then substituting positive self-talk, is a highly effective method for increasing self-esteem.

So why not give it a try?

For example, instead of saying to yourself, *I'm not good at public speaking,* a self put-down, you can now choose to say, *I'm really going to work harder on improving my public speaking skills.*

Another common example is the use of name-calling in one's self-talk such as, *I'm really an idiot when it comes to using commas in my papers.* In this case, in order to eliminate this highly negative self-criticism, you can choose to say, *Putting commas in the right places is something I'm going to work on.*

A New Beginning: Gratitude-Based Communication

Let us say that right now, this very second, someone could wave a magic wand over your head and all your self-criticism and criticism of others would vanish. As a result, it might be very silent inside your head, and your conversations might be much quieter too. Nevertheless, as you may know, *nature*  *abhors a vacuum,* so something would pop up in these silences.

How about replacing this potential void with *gratitude-based communication* or communication based on appreciation of every aspect of your life?

Gratitude-based communication is similar to the previously mentioned positive self-talk; however, it not only includes the positive mental aspects of a situation but also includes the positive emotional and physical elements. In other words, gratitude-based communication is *both* thinking and feeling positive.

Relating back to self-talk, perhaps you have said something negative like this to yourself, *It's really tough to speak to a group of people.* By using gratitude-based communication, you may now choose to say, *This will be a great opportunity to tell others about my speech topic.* This latter statement contains appreciation for a positive emotional element of the speaking situation — the "great opportunity." So, besides reflecting a type of positive thinking, this statement also contains a positive feeling — which makes the self-talk much more effective in raising your self-esteem.

Also, as a general rule, for nearly any situation in life that seems highly negative or hurtful, you can choose to say the following general phrases in your self-talk. They are derived from the appreciation you have for yourself, so they are another example of gratitude-based communication: *I can cope with this problem* or *I can deal with this.*

How can you apply gratitude-based communication to your upcoming speeches?

To help answer this question, here is an extremely dramatic example from world history. In World War II, in the Nazi concentration camps, many prisoners were sent to die in the gas chambers. After the war, we learned that a small group of Jewish prisoners were actually singing and dancing on the way to meet their deaths in these chambers. Had they gone insane? No, not at all. What these apparently cheerful inmates did was display the ultimate in gratitude-based communication. Before being led to their deaths, they decided to view the entire situation as being sent to heaven. So, when their time of execution came, they expressed their gratitude in song and dance!

If gratitude-based communication can be found in this terribly bleak situation, then it certainly can be found in your speeches.

A prime example is how you may have felt in the past moments before you were about to give a speech. Do you remember feeling some of the common symptoms of being nervous — an upset or queasy stomach, rapidly beating heart, or cold and clammy hands? Now, by using gratitude-based communication, instead of being in this kind of pain — which may have felt as though you were going to the gas chambers — you can choose to feel good, even happy, about an upcoming speech.

Here is how. Instead of repeatedly thinking about these types of physical ailments, and thereby making them worse, you can feel much happier by appreciating some of the aspects of your speaking situation. For example, a speaker can concentrate on the excitement that she has about telling the audience the latest medical discoveries regarding heart attacks. As she delivers her speech, she will then be focusing her thoughts on the high amount of enthusiasm she has about these medical miracles — and not on her worries. As a result of incorporating gratitude-based communication, some or all of her nervousness will disappear.

Gratitude-based communication is the best way to overcome your single biggest obstacle to successful public speaking — *speech anxiety* — which comes from the fear of public speaking. Chapter 10, *Eliminating Speech Anxiety,* is entirely devoted to this subject, and it contains nearly forty techniques — most of which are forms of gratitude-based communication — to help you totally eliminate your speech anxiety. If you are very concerned about your level of speech anxiety, you may read this chapter at any time.

Chapter 2
Understanding Key Terms and Definitions

Vocabulary List

Here are key theoretical terms in the field of communication that will assist you as you read the rest of the book.

Source The person who initiates and sends a message.

Message The information itself, a type of knowledge, attitude, or behavior.
Knowledge is a fact or factual level; an attitude is an opinion or belief; and a behavior is an emotional or physical experience.

Channel Any of the five senses and technology used as a means to communicate a message.

Receiver The person who decodes a message. In regard to a speech, a receiver is a listener, not a "hearer" — a person who is present but does not interpret the meaning of any of the words in a speech.

Feedback The message or messages sent by a receiver in response to a source's message.

Communication The sharing of knowledge, attitudes, or behaviors via the process of sending and receiving messages between people, or *inter*personal communication, and within a person, or *intra*personal communication.

Oral Communication Type of communication in which a source's messages are entirely composed of spoken words, or verbal communication.

Speech Communication Type of communication in which at least 51 percent of the messages from a source are composed of oral communication.

Public Speaking Type of speech communication in which a source shows at least her face to a minimum of two receivers or audience members who also — at the same time — show at least their face to the source.

Feedback from receivers is primarily based on the content of the messages from the source or speaker. Of the total messages communicated between a source and receivers, at least 51 percent originate from the source.

Speech Type of public speaking; it is the total amount of a source's messages within a specified time period.

Impromptu Speech Type of public speaking in which a source delivers her speech with little or no preparation. The time available to prepare this type of speech is 25 percent or less of the time allotted for the speech.

Prepared Speech Type of public speaking in which a source reads her speech verbatim, or word-for-word, from written information usually in the form of a script. This type of speech also may be memorized.

Extemporaneous Speech Type of public speaking in which a source delivers her speech using a Persuasive Message Strategy as her only guide, or cue, as to what to communicate.

The extemporaneous speech is the most common type of speech and contains the best aspects of the other two types: the natural, spontaneous delivery of the impromptu speech and the highly organized written format of the prepared speech.

Interview Type of speech communication in which the primary topic of a conversation is determined by a source whose messages are mostly composed of questions.

Employment Interview A type of interview in which the topic chosen by a source who is a prospective employer, or interviewer, is the evaluation of the qualifications of a receiver who is a prospective employee, or interviewee.

The most frequent channel for this type of interview is the physical presence of all sources and receivers in the same space at the same time with all participants being able to see each other's faces.

An interviewer is usually a member of the company which has the vacant position, and more than one interview can be expected for most full-time, career positions. The same interviewer may not necessarily conduct all interviews.

Communication Guide A five-step problem-solving model to totally satisfy a source's speech communication goal. The steps are called: Claim Statement, Receiver Analysis, Source Credibility Analysis, Channel Characteristics Analysis, Persuasive Message Strategy.

The Communication Guide may be used to prepare for any type of speech communication. The responses in it are very concise, usually in the form of short phrases.

Claim Statement The one sentence written and oral statement of the source's speech communication goal; it is the source's single most-desired change in her receivers.

Receiver Analysis The predictions of the receivers' most interesting knowledge, attitudes and behaviors.

Source Credibility Analysis The predictions of the most credible or believable aspects of the source through use of the Receiver Analysis.

Channel Characteristics Analysis The predictions of the most interesting communication channels through use of the Receiver Analysis.

Persuasive Message Strategy The predictions of the most interesting order of the most interesting knowledge, attitudes, and behaviors within the source's upcoming speech. It is one page and is completed by using information from the previous sections of the Communication Guide.

For an extemporaneous speech, the Persuasive Message Strategy is held in one hand or laid on a nearby lectern, desk, or table. Note cards are never used in lieu of the Persuasive Message Strategy because they require at least one hand to manage them. This greatly interferes with the speaker's ability to gesture as well as lessens the speaker's eye contact with her audience.

Fact A single idea that 99 percent of all sources and receivers are in present agreement.

Most statements by highly credible experts, such as doctors and lawyers, consist of interesting attitudes or opinions — not facts. A doctor will produce a diagnosis and suggest a "second opinion." An attorney will produce a legal opinion to persuade the same in the "opinion of the jury" or "opinion of the court."

Factual Level A single, abstract fact pertaining to two or more facts.

It is a single fact that "Chicago is a city in Illinois." "Major cities in Illinois" is a factual level statement because it pertains to at least two other facts — the cities of Chicago, Springfield, and St. Louis.

Chapter 3
Learning to Use the Communication Guide:
Five Easy Steps

Speaking without thinking is like shooting a gun without aiming.

Proverb

In other words, as a public speaker, you need to plan carefully before speaking. Otherwise, disastrous things can happen.

Here is the five-step Communication Guide, an *easy-to-learn and easy-to-use* method of planning and delivering your upcoming extemporaneous speeches — the most common type found in business and professional environments.

The following chapters will help you learn how to complete each of the five steps successfully. You also will learn how to use the Communication Guide to create prepared speeches, impromptu speeches, and succeed at employment interviews.

Communication Guide

Claim Statement (Step 1)

In terms of your receivers' knowledge, attitudes, and behaviors, what is your *single* most-desired change? Write this desired change as your claim through use of this format:

I want my receivers to primarily *know, believe,* or *do* (circle one)

_____

_____ as a result of listening to my speech.

Receiver Analysis (Step 2)

Analyze your receivers through use of the following criteria.

1. *Demographics*: In terms of your claim, how would you describe your receivers as a group?

Cultural/Physical (external traits)	*Psychological* (internal traits)
a.	a.
b.	b.
c.	c.
d.	d.
e.	e.

2. *Knowledge:* In terms of your claim, what kinds of facts or factual levels — in any order — are your receivers highly interested in? (Cue words: *knowing who, what, when, where, why, or how . . .*)

a.

b.

c.

d.

e.

3. *Attitudes:* In terms of your claim, what kinds of opinions are your receivers highly interested in? (Cue words: *believing/believing that . . .*)

    a.

    b.

    c.

    d.

    e.

4. *Behaviors:* In terms of your claim, what kinds of experiences are your receivers highly interested in? (Cue word: *experiencing an "-ing" word at the start of each answer below*)

    a.

    b.

    c.

    d.

    e.

Source Credibility Analysis (Step 3)

Analyze your source credibility through use of the following criteria.

Communicating source credibility: Using your Receiver Analysis, how do you plan to communicate high source credibility? Namely, by: *citing credentials, citing experience, citing other highly credible people, citing yourself, and citing demographics*? Please explain.

    a. Could quote/state/relate . . .

    b. Could quote/state/relate . . .

    c. Could quote/state/relate . . .

    d. Could quote/state/relate . . .

    e. Could quote/state/relate . . .

Channel Characteristics Analysis (Step 4)

Analyze your communication channels through use of the following criteria.

Channel utilization: Using your Receiver Analysis, what interesting communication channels, namely: *kinesics, haptics, visual/sensory aids, paralinguistics, chronemics, proxemics, dress, and monosensory aids* do you plan to use? Please explain.

a. Could show/give/wear . . .

b. Could show/give/wear . . .

c. Could show/give/wear . . .

d. Could show/give/wear . . .

e. Could show/give/wear . . .

Persuasive Message Strategy (Step 5)

Claim Statement: I want my receivers to primarily *know, believe,* or *do* (circle one)

_____

_____ as a result of listening to my speech.

I. Introduction. Type: _____

☐ Check this box if your claim is paraphrased and reinforced here, *or* check the box located in the conclusion.

II. Body. Check one: ☐ Inductive ☐ Deductive

The body includes at least three major points, A-C, with at least four supporting points. A-C also are kinds of behavioral-level information from your Receiver Analysis that start with " *ing*" words such as *learning, feeling, enjoying, eating, viewing,* or other similar words.

A.

    1.

    2.

    3.

    4.

B.

    1.

    2.

    3.

    4.

C.

    1.

    2.

    3.

    4.

III. Conclusion. Type: _____

☐ Check this box if your claim is paraphrased and reinforced here.

Communication Guide *(page 4 of 4)*

Sample Communication Guide

On the following page is a sample of a completed Communication Guide. By reading through the completed guide, you will get an idea of how your own guide will look when you have completed it.

You may notice that the last step, the Persuasive Message Strategy, is similar to a keyword outline. However, there are major differences, that will be explained in Chapter 8.

Communication Guide

Claim Statement (Step 1)

In terms of your receivers' knowledge, attitudes, and behaviors, what is your *single* most-desired change? Write this desired change as your claim through use of this format:

I want my receivers to primarily (know,) believe, or *do* (circle one)

what it is like to live in Tucson, Arizona

_____ as a result of listening to my speech.

Receiver Analysis (Step 2)

Analyze your receivers through use of the following criteria.

1. *Demographics*: In terms of your claim, how would you describe your receivers as a group?

Cultural/Physical (external traits)	*Psychological* (internal traits)
a. 1 person is a past visitor to Tucson	a. Most know little about Tucson
b. Most have lived in Chicago their entire lives	b. Some like mountains
c. All work full-time	c. Almost all are very interested
d. Some have visited the Grand Canyon	d. Some are impulsive
e. None are Latino	e. All but 3 are open-minded

2. *Knowledge:* In terms of your claim, what kinds of facts or factual levels — in any order — are your receivers highly interested in? (Cue words: *knowing who, what, when, where, why, or how . . .*)

a. Who the current residents of Tucson are

b. What the cost of living is

c. When the best time to visit is

d. Where it is located

e. Why one lives there

f. How to visit

Communication Guide (page 1 of 4)

3. *Attitudes:* In terms of your claim, what kinds of opinions are your receivers highly interested in? (Cue words: *believing/believing that . . .*)

   a. Tucson has great places to visit

   b. Tucson is one of the sunniest cities in the country

   c. Tucson is peaceful and relaxing

   d. Tucson has great Mexican food

   e. Tucson is still part of the "Old West"

4. *Behaviors:* In terms of your claim, what kinds of experiences are your receivers highly interested in? (Cue word: *experiencing an "-ing" word at the start of each answer below*)

   a. Enjoy*ing* summer every day

   b. See*ing* beautiful mountain views

   c. Be*ing* a part of the "Old West"

   d. Feel*ing* charmed by the unique Sonoran desert lifestyle

   e. Learn*ing* about the booming economy

Source Credibility Analysis (Step 3)

Analyze your source credibility through use of the following criteria.

Communicating source credibility: Using your Receiver Analysis, how do you plan to communicate high source credibility? Namely, by: *citing credentials, citing experience, citing other highly credible people, citing yourself, and citing demographics*? Please explain.

   a. Could (quote)/state/relate . . . University of Arizona studies, 9/06, on the increase in tourism in Tucson

   b. Could quote/(state)/relate . . . that I was a resident of Tucson for 15 years

   c. Could (quote)/state/relate . . . John Zipperstein, writer, *Tucson Magazine*, in a 10/06 issue on the sunny and warm weather all year

   d. Could quote/(state)/relate . . . that I have been a travel agent for Travel One in Chicago for 2 years

   e. Could quote/state/(relate) . . . my fun experiences visiting the Arizona Sonora Desert Museum (6 years) and hiking Sabino Canyon (10 years)

Channel Characteristics Analysis (Step 4)

Analyze your communication channels through use of the following criteria.

Channel utilization: Using your Receiver Analysis, what interesting communication channels, namely: *kinesics, haptics, visual/sensory aids, paralinguistics, chronemics, proxemics, dress, and monosensory aids* do you plan to use? Please explain.

a. Could show/give/wear . . . at least 3 samples of cacti found in Tucson, including a picture of the giant Saguaro cactus

b. Could show/give/wear . . . slides of my visits to the top tourist attractions and great Sonoran desert views in Tucson

c. Could show/give/wear . . . my work attire: button-down shirt with Travel One logo, khaki dress slacks, and Chicago Chamber of Commerce pin

d. Could show/give/wear . . . 2 or 3 posters of spectacular Tucson mountain views right behind me as I speak to keep attention on my speech

e. Could show/give/wear . . . brochures from the Tucson Chamber of Commerce describing the lifestyle in Tucson

Persuasive Message Strategy (Step 5)

Claim Statement: I want my receivers to primarily ⟨*know*⟩ *believe*, or *do* (circle one)

_____what it is like to live in Tucson, Arizona_____

_____ as a result of listening to my speech.

I. Introduction. Type: _Poignant Story_____

☐ Check this box if your claim is paraphrased and reinforced here, *or* check the box located in the conclusion.

II. Body. Check one: ☑ Inductive ☐ Deductive

The body includes at least three major points, A-C, with at least four supporting points. A-C also are kinds of behavioral-level information from your Receiver Analysis that start with "-ing" words such as *learning, feeling, enjoying, eating, viewing,* or other similar words.

A. Enjoy*ing* summer every day

    1. Lived in Tucson 15 years   5. Great Mexican food

    2. Travel agent   6. 1 hour from Mexico – map

    3. Where it is located – map

    4. John Zipperstein, *Tucson Magazine*

B. Feel*ing* charmed by the unique Sonoran desert lifestyle

    1. Peaceful and relaxing – cacti

    2. Seeing beautiful mountain views – slides

    3. Being a part of the "Old West" – slides

    4. Great places to visit – slides

C. Gett*ing* an inside look at the economy

    1. University of Arizona studies

    2. Chamber of Commerce – brochures

    3. Growth rate in population

    4. Why one lives there

III. Conclusion. Type: _Cool Quote_____

☑ Check this box if your claim is paraphrased and reinforced here.

         Communication Guide (page 4 of 4)

Chapter 4
Creating Your Claim Statement:
Step One

What Is Your Claim Statement?

Step One in your Communication Guide is the process of creating your *claim statement* or claim. As you may recall, this is the written and spoken one sentence statement of your *single most-desired change* in your receivers.

According to psychologists, this change can be any one of these three types:

Changes in your receivers' *knowledge, attitudes,* or *behaviors*

There Are Three Kinds of Claims

knowledge claim changing your receivers' facts or factual levels in one way

attitudinal claim changing your receivers' opinions or beliefs in one way

behavioral claim changing your receivers' emotional or physical experiences in one way

Other synonyms for the term claim statement include your main idea, your most important point, and the major idea you want to get across. Obviously, these are less accurate in a scientific sense; however, they still help convey the general idea of the definition of a claim.

As for the three kinds of claim statements themselves, there are some interesting differences. In general, the level of difficulty in communicating the statements increases in the following order: knowledge claims, attitudinal claims, and behavioral claims. And, our economic system pays or rewards its workers in increasing amounts in the same order. In other words, the more you can change the behavior of other people, the more you are likely to get paid.

The same person also can have conflicting knowledge, attitudinal, and behavioral claims. For example, a person can accept the fact that she is on a diet (knowledge claim), believe that a hot fudge sundae with whipped cream and a cherry is fattening (attitudinal claim), yet still perform a behavior — eat an ice cream sundae (behavioral claim) — which is inconsistent with the previous two claims.

William James, the famous Harvard professor and psychologist, was reported to have stated that he could lecture to his students for more than an hour and get only one point — his claim — across. Was it because James was an inept speaker or that his students were unintelligent? No. It was because *most of us think more than two and one-half times as fast as a speaker can talk,* and our minds are constantly wandering. It is as though we have a remote control inside our head, and we are always channel surfing for something more interesting. And, as you may have experienced, if something that you view is not extremely interesting, then off your mind goes to some other point of possible interest. So, in your speeches, strive to make everything you say and do, even every breath you take, be as interesting as possible to communicate your claim successfully.

And finally, besides being interesting, your claim must be concisely communicated. How so? Imagine someone about to get on an elevator and having to quickly summarize what your entire speech is about — just as the elevator doors begin to close. This scenario illustrates the kind of economy of words that are necessary for an effective claim statement.

Method

To make your claim for your speech, answer these three questions:

1. *What is something I know a lot about?*

2. *What is something I strongly believe in?*

3. *What is something I very much want others to do or experience?*

The reasoning behind these questions is that an effective speech needs to come from something you deeply know, profoundly believe in, or strongly want others to do or experience. Otherwise, you would probably be speaking on something you do not know much about, do not really believe in, or do not genuinely want others to do or experience. *A speech based on that low level of information would not make much sense, would it?*

Therefore, if one general subject or idea comes to you as an answer to all three questions, or at least two of them, you should use that particular subject to help create your claim statement. However, if you answered all three questions differently, then choose the one most interesting answer to convert to your claim statement.

How do you specifically write your claim statement?

Just narrow the choice you made to *one* observable and measurable fact or factual level, opinion, or experience that you strongly want to communicate. Then, if this is a knowledge claim, circle the word "know" in your claim statement. If it is an attitudinal claim, circle the word "believe" in the claim statement. Or, if it is a behavioral claim, circle the word "do" in the claim statement, and add the words "agree to" after "do." The reason for adding "agree to" is to remind you that changing your receivers' behavior is based on choice, not coercion or force. After all, when you are persuaded to buy a product or service, you usually are asked to sign a document called a sales *agreement* that verifies your choice in the matter.

The following are some sample claim statements. By reading these, you can get an idea of what yours needs to look like. For easier reading, the beginning, "I want my receivers to primarily know, believe, or do," and the ending, "as a result of listening to my speech," have been omitted.

⟩ Knowledge Claims

Begin with *who, what, when, where, why,* or *how* — the 5 ws + h.

> *Who* the primary consumers of Nike shoes are
> *What* the Shanti Foundation is
> *When* to sign up to give blood
> *Where* to recycle your old clothing
> *Why* children need to be taught how to cope with violence
> *How* to prevent foot odor

⟩ Attitudinal Claims

Are composed of statements that *fewer than* 99 percent of people agree on — opinions and beliefs.

> Investing in mutual funds is a great way to save for retirement
> Being a hostess at Red Lobster is a tough job
> Eldercare is a rewarding experience
> Paper covers for compact discs are better than plastic ones
> Euthanasia should not be considered a sin in the Catholic religion
> A wild horse is the best type for endurance racing
> Serial killers are a real threat to society
> Accutane is a short-term treatment plan that cures acne

⟩ Behavioral Claims

Begin with the words *agree to* followed by a verb or verbs stating the desired action.

> *Agree to* consider starting a Neighborhood Watch program
> *Agree to* sign up to give blood next Tuesday at school
> *Agree to* volunteer for the Cook County March of Dimes walk
> *Agree to* apply for a Sears charge account
> *Agree to* buy my Ford Mustang
> *Agree to* try Tempo gum
> *Agree to* donate $10 to the U.S. Holocaust Memorial Museum
> *Agree to* buy a Timex watch

Getting Started

Complete your claim statement by using this replica of the first section from the Communication Guide:

Claim Statement (Step 1)

In terms of your receivers' knowledge, attitudes, and behaviors, what is your *single* most-desired change? Write this desired change as your claim through use of this format:

I want my receivers to primarily *know, believe,* or *do* (circle one)

_____

_____ as a result of listening to my speech.

Checking Your Work

Interested in checking your claim statement to see whether it is the type you want?

All you have to do is read your statement three times, first as a knowledge claim using "know" as your verb, second as an attitudinal claim using "believe" as your verb, and last as a behavioral claim using "experience" in lieu of the word "do" as your verb (substituting "experience" for "do" facilitates the semantics).

Here is how this test works. Of the three claim statements you just read — either aloud or to yourself — the one that simply sounded the most correct, usually is. Also, to ensure that your claim statement is the right type, have someone else, someone who has at least some communication experience, read your claim. If this receiver agrees that your claim statement is the type you intended, then you probably have created your claim correctly.

When you are satisfied with your work, transfer your claim to a blank Communication Guide located in the Appendix.

Chapter 5
Creating Your Receiver Analysis:
Step Two

Which Level Is Best?

Do you remember the Venn diagrams that you looked at in Chapter 1?

The following ones are similar, yet this time there is an important difference. To see this difference, answer this question: Which of these three Venn diagrams represents the *best* level of speech communication?

Is it level 1 in which the circle on the left, representing you as the source, and the circle on the right, representing your receivers, are separate?

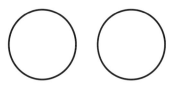

Is it level 2 in which the two circles previously mentioned slightly overlap?

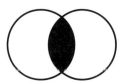

Or, is it level 3 in which the two circles almost completely overlap?

If you remembered that communication is sharing, then you chose level 3 in which nearly everything you said was shared with almost everything your receivers listened to. In other words, in level 3, nearly perfect communication occurred.

Here are some follow-up questions: In terms of being considered "interesting" by your receivers, in which level would you, the source, be considered by your receivers as most interesting: level 1, 2, or 3? Why?

If you answered level 3 again, you are correct. The reason is that, given there was no coercion or threat involved, your receivers demonstrated, by their choice, the level in which their interest was highest — level 3. Now the key question for you, as someone about to prepare an effective speech, is *How can I achieve level 3 communication — the best level — in my upcoming speech?*

The answer? By effectively completing the *Receiver Analysis* in your Communication Guide. In this step, based on your receivers' demographics, you make predictions about the knowledge, attitudes, and behaviors that they — not you — find most interesting. The more accurate your choice of these predictions for your speech, the more interesting you are likely to be and the more likely you will communicate your claim with level 3 accuracy.

Making Your Receiver Analysis

To begin your Receiver Analysis, Step Two of the Communication Guide, answer the first question requiring the demographics of your receivers.

Demographics are the *cultural, physical, and psychological characteristics of a group of receivers*. List five cultural and physical characteristics and five psychological characteristics. Because each demographic is a prediction, include an estimate of the number of receivers who fall under each type. In general, terms such as "none," "some," "most," and "all" will suffice. If actual numbers or percentages can be ascertained, that is even better.

Sample Demographic Analysis

Here is an example of a completed Demographics section of the Receiver Analysis. It appears first because these demographics will function as your *clues* to predicting the rest of the answers in your Receiver Analysis.

Receiver Analysis (Step 2)

Analyze your receivers through use of the following criteria.

1. *Demographics*: In terms of your claim, how would you describe your receivers as a group?

Cultural/Physical (external traits)	*Psychological* (internal traits)
a. 1 person is a past visitor to Tucson	a. Most know little about Tucson
b. Most have lived in Chicago their entire lives	b. Some like mountains
c. All work full-time	c. Almost all are very interested
d. Some have visited the Grand Canyon	d. Some are impulsive
e. None are Latino	e. All but 3 are open-minded

Which Demographics to Choose?

Cultural demographics such as "marital status" and physical demographics such as "race" are *external* traits of a group of receivers, and the predictions of these traits can be derived from observations of your receivers.

Psychological demographics such as "self-esteem" are the invisible *internal* traits of a group, and the predictions of these traits can be: (1) inferred from your receivers' cultural and physical demographics or (2) determined by a special type of survey, interview, or test of your receivers.

Look over the following list of highly significant demographics, then choose the ones that are most relevant to your claim:

Cultural/Physical	*Psychological*
Age	Open-minded
Sex	Close-minded
Sexual orientation	High intelligence
Race	Low intelligence
Income	High self-esteem
Ethnic background	Low self-esteem
Marital status	Extroverted
Religion	Introverted
Education	Abstract thinking
Social class	Concrete thinking
Occupation	Idealistic
Geographic location	Realistic
Physical characteristics	Rational
National origin	Emotional
Lineage	Theoretical
Ancestry .	Practical
Parentage	Aggressive
Nationality	Passive
Birthplace	Happy
Health	Sad
Citizenship	Thoughtful
Family relationships	Impulsive
Military	Hardworking
Clubs	Lazy
Societies	*Others:* Friendly, unfriendly, kind, unkind,
Political affiliations	interested, apathetic, honest, dishonest, generous, frugal, sensitive, insensitive, fair,
Sports activities	unfair, patient, impatient, religious, irreligious,
Social activities	likeable, dislikeable, optimistic, pessimistic, attractive, unattractive, safe, fearful,
Community service activities	sympathetic, unsympathetic, quick, slow

If these do not result in a useful set of demographics of your receivers, then you will need to seek more relevant ones.

For example, for the claim "how to train a dog to do tricks," the cultural demographic of "political affiliations" is not highly significant. Another demographic needs to be researched. In this case, a more relevant demographic, such as "dog owners," which would refer to the amount of receivers who currently own a dog, would be much more useful in creating predictions related to this claim about dog training.

The same logic applies to psychological demographics. Let us say that the claim is "the benefits of being a vegetarian." A more specific psychological demographic such as "liking the taste of salad" would provide much more helpful information than the demographic "extroverted." Therefore this new demographic should be used instead.

After completing the Demographics question, answer the next three questions in your Receiver Analysis — numbers 2, 3, and 4.

You may notice that at the end of each of these questions there are a set of cue words starting with either *knowing, believing,* or *experiencing.* You can use these to help you sound out each of your predictions for accuracy. This technique is the same one you used to test your claim statement.

If you wish, you can conduct a poll or survey of your receivers using the questions themselves. For example, for the claim "the benefits of being a vegetarian," the speaker could pass out a survey with the following paraphrase of the second question: "What kinds of facts are you highly interested in regarding the benefits of being a vegetarian?" If the speaker decides that the responses to such a survey are reliable, then she could use these as actual answers in her Receiver Analysis.

Here is an example of how to complete the rest of the Receiver Analysis:

---

2. *Knowledge:* In terms of your claim, what kinds of facts or factual levels — in any order — are your receivers highly interested in? (Cue words: *knowing who, what, when, where, why, or how . . .*)

   a. Who the current residents of Tucson are

   b. What the cost of living is

   c. When the best time to visit is

   d. Where it is located

   e. Why one lives there

   f. How to visit

3. *Attitudes:* In terms of your claim, what kinds of opinions are your receivers highly interested in? (Cue words: *believing/believing that . . .*)

   a. Tucson has great places to visit

---

b. Tucson is one of the sunniest cities in the country

c. Tucson is peaceful and relaxing

d. Tucson has great Mexican food

e. Tucson is still part of the "Old West"

4. *Behaviors:* In terms of your claim, what kinds of experiences are your receivers highly interested in? (Cue word: *experiencing an "-ing" word at the start of each answer below*)

a. Enjoy*ing* summer every day

b. See*ing* beautiful mountain views

c. Be*ing* a part of the "Old West"

d. Feel*ing* charmed by the unique Sonoran desert lifestyle

e. Learn*ing* about the booming economy

It is now time to complete your demographic analysis and answer the three questions based on the analysis. Remember, this is the most important step in achieving level 3 communication.

To complete the Receiver Analysis for your claim, use the same blank Communication Guide in the Appendix that you used to create your Claim Statement.

Chapter 6
Creating Your Source Credibility Analysis:
Step Three

The Single Most . . .

Do you know what is the *single most persuasive element* in the speech communication process?

It is *source credibility,* or how believable or persuasive you are as perceived by your receivers. In simpler terms, as Winston Churchill explained, source credibility is not what you say or how you say it but *who you are.*

In your Communication Guide, Step Three is your Source Credibility Analysis. This is the process you follow to predict what the most believable and persuasive knowledge, attitudes, and behaviors are regarding you as the speaker or source.

Have you thought about where your source credibility comes from? Just as *beauty is in the eye of the beholder,* so is source credibility. In other words, you do not determine your source credibility, but it is *your receivers' perceptions of you* that determine your source credibility.

You may already know the supreme importance of source credibility. Perhaps you have heard the adage that advises you to *Consider the source* before you evaluate information. In support of this, researchers have discovered that source credibility is so powerful an element in speech communication that, in general, the higher a speaker's source credibility, the more persuasive a speaker's speech.

Here are some additional examples of the power of source credibility. In our court system, who usually wins the case — the most persuasive or the most truthful legal representative? Always, the winner is the person who is *perceived* as the most truthful — the one with the highest source credibility — who, as you may know, is not necessarily the most truthful. Think about the election process. Who wins a political election, the best candidate or the one who appears, by her pre-election communication of her source credibility, to be the best candidate? . . . Is the answer obvious now?

Furthermore, in college, when an undergraduate student passes a class, she earns a certain amount of credits. Notice the same root word in *credit* as in source *credibility,* namely, *cred.* If this same student then passes a group of classes that are considered a program, she earns a credential — usually an Associate's or Bachelor's degree. Again, did you notice the same root word in *credential* as credit? It is no coincidence, because all three words — credit, credential, and source credibility — share the idea of increasing how believable or persuasive a person is. So, one of the most important reasons that a student spends a large amount of time, energy, and money on a college education is to greatly increase source credibility.

In whose eyes might a student want to be perceived with her new high source credibility?

How about a prospective employer? When an applicant presents a resume that lists a college degree, the applicant wants a prospective employer to believe that her claim, "you should hire me," is the *most credible* claim compared to the same claim from all other applicants. If the prospective employer agrees with her, then she will be hired. All the effort that she expended on her college education will be worthwhile!

Even after a student is hired, she would still want to communicate high source credibility. As a new employee making a proposal, she could say, *I have a Bachelor's degree in business; therefore, you should believe me that . . . .*

Speaking of higher education, why do teachers often ask students to quote library sources for essays, reports, and other similar assignments?

Because associating the claim of a student with ideas from other highly credible authors increases that student's source credibility. Therefore, teachers ask students to build their source credibility by quoting highly credible authors whose information is found in books, magazines, and encyclopedias, which are conveniently located in libraries.

These authors usually possess an educational credential and many years of experience. That is why they are called "experts." However, there are people without a college degree who also may be considered an expert. These people have achieved high source credibility in other ways, and these ways, or techniques, are explained in the next part of the chapter.

And finally, if you consider source credibility at the psychological level, according to communication researchers, it consists of three main personality traits:

1. *Expertness* — how knowledgeable, skilled, or trained a person appears

2. *Trustworthiness* — how kind, just, or fair a person appears

3. *Dynamism* — how energetic, forceful, or bold a person appears

Certain obvious traits such as good looks and attractiveness, in general, do not affect your source credibility unless, of course, your speech is on a subject such as makeup, personal grooming, or other appearance-related factors. So, when you are preparing your speech, you do not need to consider cosmetic surgery or adopting a new personality — just concern yourself with the following highly effective techniques to increase your expertness, trustworthiness, and dynamism.

Making Your Source Credibility Analysis

Here is a list of techniques and suggestions on how to communicate high source credibility.

Techniques	Suggestions
Citing Your Credentials	State the following types of credentials that you possess: educational degrees, educational certifications, educational classes completed, awards, honors, accomplishments, achievements, seminars completed, licenses, permits, and medals. For example, a speaker may say that *I have earned a Bachelor of Science degree in chemical engineering from the University of Chicago* when her claim is "what renewable sources of energy are available in the twenty-first century."
Citing Your Experience	State the following types of experience that you have in number of years, beginning with a minimum of one-quarter year: work experience, life experience, age, past experience with your receivers, past experience with your claim, previous reputation, family experience, military experience, community service experience, activities, interests, proficiencies, travel, and hobbies. For example, a speaker might say that she has been the district manager of Circuit City for two years when her claim is "how to shop for a personal computer."
Citing Other Highly Credible People	Highly credible people, or people who are experts, include scientists, doctors, lawyers, authors, teachers, professors, government officials, religious leaders, and prominent business executives. Besides these individuals, you can quote anyone so long as you use the techniques listed here to show why your source should be considered as highly credible.
	Who is the *most persuasive* within the above list of highly credible sources? This is the person or group who you predict possesses the most: (1) credentials,

45

Techniques	Suggestions
(Citing Other Highly Credible People, cont.)	(2) relevant experience, and (3) up-to-date information. In regard to the last trait, if a speech is based on information such as court rulings and government actions, a speaker may need to wait until just minutes before her speech to select the best source.
	State quotes from your choice of highly credible people who support your claim. A quote includes: *the source of the quote, the media in which you found the quote, the date of the quote, and the quote itself* — not necessarily in that order. For example, for the claim "eating the right food will prolong your life," a speaker may say, *According to Dr. Michael Richardson in his 2005 book, Natural Medications, You can prevent many illnesses by proper diet.*
	If you plan to quote from an unpublished source, then state: *the source of the quote, where the quote was made, the date of the quote, and the quote itself* — not necessarily in that order. For example, for the claim "you should try a weekend vacation in Tucson, Arizona," the speaker may say, *John Rogers, director of the Tucson Chamber of Commerce, said that Tucson is one of the best places to visit in the country at the national Chamber of Commerce convention held on February 20, 2005, in Chicago.*
	Besides using a *verbatim* or word-for-word quote, you can also choose to cite an expert's opinion by *paraphrasing* — using your choice of words that mean the same thing as — the information in the quote. Of these two methods, which one is best? Review your Receiver Analysis, and the answer is the one that is most interesting to your receivers.
Citing Yourself	State self-opinions that support your belief in your high source credibility. For example, the speaker may say, *I believe*

Techniques	Suggestions
(Citing Yourself, cont.)	*that I am highly expert in microchip technology* when her claim is "how to build a microchip." Or, when the claim is "buy one of my homemade sub sandwiches," the speaker may say, *In my opinion, I make the best sub sandwiches that you will ever taste.*
	The main reason for citing yourself is that your self-perception is a highly valid way of maximizing your source credibility. In general, the higher your stated self-opinion, the higher your source credibility — as well as the reverse.
Citing Demographics	State your highly credible group memberships that are interesting to your receivers. For example, if the speaker is a divorced mother of two and a member of a single parents' group, mentioning both of these in her speech adds credibility to the claim that "the Department of Social Services should increase benefits to single parents."
	Also, by including the amount of time as a group member, you can increase your source credibility even more. For example, the speaker may state that she has been a member of the Illinois Association of Broadcasters for *ten years* when the claim is "the new cable regulations in Chicago."

Sample Source Credibility Analysis

To help you understand how to use these techniques, here is an example of a completed Source Credibility Analysis. Note that the directions remind you to complete this section while you always keep in mind the interests of your receivers — your Receiver Analysis.

Source Credibility Analysis (Step 3)

Analyze your source credibility through use of the following criteria.

Communicating source credibility: Using your Receiver Analysis, how do you plan to communicate high source credibility? Namely, by: *citing credentials, citing experience, citing other highly credible people, citing yourself, and citing demographics*? Please explain.

a. Could (quote)/state/relate . . . University of Arizona studies, 9/06, on the increase in tourism in Tucson

b. Could quote/(state)/relate . . . that I was a resident of Tucson for 15 years

c. Could (quote)/state/relate . . . John Zipperstein, writer, *Tucson Magazine*, in a 10/06 issue on the sunny and warm weather all year

d. Could quote/(state)/relate . . . that I have been a travel agent for Travel One in Chicago for 2 years

e. Could quote/state/(relate) . . . my fun experiences visiting the Arizona Sonora Desert Museum (6 years) and hiking Sabino Canyon (10 years)

You may return to the Communication Guide that you have started. You are now ready to make your Source Credibility Analysis by using the techniques, suggestions, and examples in this chapter.

Chapter 7
Creating Your Channel Characteristics Analysis:
Step Four

Which Sense?

Step Four in your Communication Guide is the *Channel Characteristic Analysis*.

A "channel" is the *means* of communicating your message, namely, the use of any or all of the five senses as well as technology such as an overhead, PowerPoint graphics, a whiteboard, or a videotape presentation as a way to communicate your speech.

Or, to put it simply, a channel is not what you say, but *how* you say it.

Funny things can happen if you confuse a message with the channel used to communicate it. For example, a person is upset about something that was reported on the television news. In anger, she throws her television set out the window. In this instance, she has confused the message, a distressing news story, with the channel or medium — her television set.

A scenario from thousands of years ago also illustrates this fallacy of *confusing the medium with the message*. Rulers in ancient Rome previously received their news from skilled runners who acted as human communication channels. These runners never knew what messages they were carrying in their scrolls. When a king opened one of these scrolls and read good news, then these strong and athletic runners experienced royal treatment — fine food, drink, and other luxuries. However, if a king received bad news, perhaps about an impending invasion, then these unlucky and uninformed runners were summarily executed. As you may have guessed, from these latter consequences comes the popular admonition, *If you don't like the message, don't kill the messenger!*

Of the five senses, which one do you think is most persuasive? Hearing? Tasting? Touching? Seeing? Smelling? The answer, according to communication researchers, is seeing, or the sight channel. Indeed, these experts have verified the common adage that *Seeing is believing*.

Medical research on the brain supports this as well. If the sound of one of your speeches was so loud that every nerve fiber related to hearing in your receivers' brains was activated — about fifty thousand — that would still have only one-fortieth of the effect of a bold and expressive picture because the nerve fibers for sight are about two million.

Even more dramatic evidence comes from research done at the Arizona School for the Deaf and the Blind. When students who were both blind and deaf were asked, *Of the five senses, which one is most persuasive?* every single student answered, *Sight*.

Follow-up questions revealed that these students, without the ability to see and hear, had primarily relied on *mental pictures that were created in their head* as their most believable sense. So even when a person can only see the visual images in her brain, the sense of sight is still the most persuasive when compared to the rest of the senses!

What does this mean for effective speech communication? Quite simply, in your upcoming speeches, use as many sight channels or channels that appeal to the sense of sight as possible.

Making Your Channel Characteristics Analysis

Here is a list of channels and suggestions on how to use them in the Channel Characteristics Analysis section of your Communication Guide.

Channels	Suggestions
Kinesics *(Body language)*	Use interesting gestures and facial expressions with direct eye contact. Smile at least once — more often, if possible.
Haptics *(Touching receivers)*	Touch your receivers in interesting ways. The largest organ in the human body is the skin, so it is highly accessible to the touch channel. For example, if a speaker needs a volunteer, she can touch one of her receivers lightly on the shoulder and politely ask for that person's participation.
Visual/Sensory Aids *(Channels that mainly involve the sense of sight; other senses are involved tangentially. There are three main types.)*	
1. Animate Visual/Sensory Aids	Use visual/sensory aids composed of interesting people and animals: role-playing, skits, simulations, interviews, characterizations, endorsements, demonstrations, dramatizations, receiver participation, models, exhibits, examples, samples, and interactive video.
2. Inanimate Visual/Sensory Aids	Use visual/sensory aids composed of interesting things: photographs, digital images, tables, diagrams, charts, graphs, maps, drawings, models, sketches, cartoons, computer graphics, handouts — brochures, information, images, DVD and videotape presentations, chalkboard, dry erase board, digital whiteboard, film, slides, posters, opaque projector images, exhibits,

Channels	Suggestions
(Inanimate Visual/ Sensory Aids, cont.)	simulations, demonstrations, samples, computer programs and games, CD and cassette music, sound effects, radio, television, and records.
3. Language Visual/Sensory Aids	Use visual/sensory aids composed of interesting word construction techniques: analogies, metaphors, similes, personal stories, illustrations, examples, dialogue, actual names of receivers, specific detail about situations, concrete and familiar words — avoid jargon and abstractions, vivid verbal contrasts, anecdotes, the *you approach* in which all receivers are addressed as "you" so they feel that the speaker is communicating on a one-to-one basis with each of them, and "word-pictures" — words highly connected to the visual sense.
Paralinguistics *(Sound and meaning of the voice)*	To avoid sounding monotone and boring, use natural inflection — different tones in your voice that result from the different feelings that you have about the words you are saying. Speak with a volume of voice that is audible for all receivers without having to shout (unless needed for a speech).
Chronemics *(Time management)*	Use an interesting pace of speaking and add pauses throughout your speech to emphasize interesting ideas. Remember that your receivers will reduce their attention dramatically when you speak past the allotted time limit. So, to remain interesting, speak within the agreed upon time limits.
Proxemics *(Organization of the speaking venue)*	Change the physical elements in the speech environment in the most interesting ways. The most important elements are: (1) location of the speaker, (2) seating arrangement of receivers, (3) location of lectern or podium, (4) location of visual/sensory aids, (5) amount and type of lighting, (6) air temperature setting, and (7) location of microphone.

Channels	Suggestions
Dress *(Clothing and physical appearance)*	Dress with the attire that is most interesting to your receivers. This is either the same or different dress as your receivers. If different dress, it also needs to help communicate your claim.
	For example, for the claim "tennis is easy to learn," the speaker may wear a visor cap, athletic shirt, skirt, sweat socks, and tennis shoes — totally different attire as her audience, a typical group of students. However, when she demonstrates how to make a forehand, one of the basic strokes of tennis, her outfit will allow her to move her body more easily, hence helping communicate her claim more effectively.
Monosensory Aid (One sense only)	Use monosensory aids to increase interest in your speech. For example, for the claim "meditation reduces stress," the speaker may ask her receivers to close their eyes — thus eliminating all senses but one — and play an audiotape of a relaxing environment as she explains the benefits of meditation.

Sample Channel Characteristics Analysis

Here is an example of how a completed Channel Characteristics Analysis looks using the techniques that you have just read.

Channel Characteristics Analysis (Step 4)

Analyze your communication channels through use of the following criteria.

Channel utilization: Using your Receiver Analysis, what interesting communication channels, namely: *kinesics, haptics, visual/sensory aids, paralinguistics, chronemics, proxemics, dress, and monosensory aids* do you plan to use? Please explain.

a. Could (show)/give/wear . . . at least 3 samples of cacti found in Tucson, including a picture of the giant Saguaro cactus

b. Could (show)/give/wear . . . slides of my visits to the top tourist attractions and great Sonoran desert views in Tucson

---

c. Could show/give/wear . . . my work attire: button-down shirt with Travel One logo, khaki dress slacks, and Chicago Chamber of Commerce pin

d. Could show/give/wear . . . 2 or 3 posters of spectacular Tucson mountain views right behind me as I speak to keep attention on my speech

e. Could show/give/wear . . . brochures from the Tucson Chamber of Commerce describing the lifestyle in Tucson

Now return to your Channel Characteristics Analysis in the Appendix, and complete it using as many visual/sensory aids as possible.

Chapter 8
Creating Your Persuasive Message Strategy:
Step Five

The Most Interesting Mix

Up to this point in the Communication Guide, what you have done is similar to preparing a salad. You have gathered, cut, and sorted the necessary ingredients — the lettuce, tomatoes, carrots, and cucumbers. These ingredients are laid out in front of you in neat little piles called the Claim Statement, Receiver Analysis, Source Credibility Analysis, and Channel Characteristics Analysis.

In this chapter, you will learn how to mix all these elements together in the *most interesting way* — Step Five, the *Persuasive Message Strategy*.

At first blush, the Persuasive Message Strategy resembles a keyword outline. However, the Persuasive Message Strategy is much more effective for two reasons: (1) it is based on the previous four sections of the Communication Guide and (2) it is created using a method that incorporates the latest speech communication research.

Background

The information in the one page Persuasive Message Strategy is written as concisely as possible, usually as one or two words or as very short phrases. As an extemporaneous speech is being delivered, a speaker glances at these verbal cues starting with the introduction at the top of the page. As the speech progresses, the speaker proceeds to glance downward at these cues until she reaches the bottom of the page or the end of the conclusion. After a speaker reads each verbal cue, she creates at least one or two sentences that will express the main idea of the verbal cue.

Here is an example of this process. The speaker looks at major point "A" in her Persuasive Message Strategy and then says a sentence or two. After that, she glances at point "1," the point right underneath point A, and then says another sentence or two. If a visual/sensory aid is listed in the Persuasive Message Strategy by the use of a hyphen (as shown), then the speaker's sentences also will need to include the explanation or use of this visual/sensory aid. When a speaker very confidently knows what the next points are, such as points "2" and "3" listed under point A and point 1, then — *without looking at these points* — she says a sentence or two regarding these points. In general, a speaker only looks at the Persuasive Message Strategy when she needs to be reminded of the order or content of the sentences in her speech. Otherwise, a speaker very confidently delivers her speech with the Persuasive Message Strategy located close enough to be easily read in case she forgets an aspect of her speech.

As a speaker learns to glance less often at the Persuasive Message Strategy, she can begin to concentrate on another aspect regarding her delivery: the reactions or feedback from her audience. By using this information, she can make unplanned improvements in her upcoming sentences — a unique advantage of the extemporaneous type of public speaking.

For example, for the claim, "marijuana should be legalized as a controlled substance," a speaker may notice that most of her receivers' faces appear very surprised by "the many health benefits of marijuana use" that she has stated. She did not plan for this type of response; however, since this is an extemporaneous speech, she may consider the receivers' feedback and make improvements in her speech.

In this case, she may add the following sentences which increase her credibility regarding her recent statements: *You might be interested in knowing that my research on the health benefits of marijuana comes from Dr. Barbara Powell, a professor in the University of Michigan Medical School. She has over twenty years' experience studying the medical effects of marijuana and is the author of over five books on the subject.*

As for how to deal with a verbatim quote of a highly credible source, only the name of the person or organization needs to be written in the Persuasive Message Strategy. Then when a speaker sees one of these names as she is delivering her speech, the quote is recited from profound personal experience ("by heart"). A speaker may also paraphrase or summarize a quote, but it should never be read directly from the Persuasive Message Strategy. This latter method is highly uninteresting for receivers.

What can you do if you feel that you must read a quote verbatim? In this instance, you may make a written copy of the quote, perhaps in the form of a chart or handout. Then, as you read the quote, your audience can follow along with you, instead of watching you read the quote yourself.

Nevertheless, some speeches are read to an audience — the so-called prepared speeches. For a prepared speech, the Persuasive Message Strategy is created in the exact same way as for the extemporaneous speech. The only difference is that for a prepared speech, the Persuasive Message Strategy is used to write the entire speech before it is delivered.

As for the impromptu speech, no Persuasive Message Strategy is used — a speaker does not have enough time to use this formal process. However, enough time does exist for another method that uses the Communication Guide. So you will be ready for an impromptu speech, this method is presented at the end of this chapter.

Sample Persuasive Message Strategy

The following is an example of a Persuasive Message Strategy. It completes the model that we have been using throughout the book.

Persuasive Message Strategy (Step 5)

Claim Statement: I want my receivers to primarily (know,) believe, or do (circle one)

what it is like to live in Tucson, Arizona

_____ as a result of listening to my speech.

I. Introduction. Type: _Poignant Story_

☐ Check this box if your claim is paraphrased and reinforced here, *or* check the box located in the conclusion.

II. Body. Check one: ☑Inductive ☐Deductive

The body includes at least three major points, A-C, with at least four supporting points. A-C also are kinds of behavioral-level information from your Receiver Analysis that start with " *ing*" words such as *learning, feeling, enjoying, eating, viewing,* or other similar words.

    A. Enjoy*ing* summer every day

        1. Lived in Tucson 15 years   5. Great Mexican food

        2. Travel agent   6. 1 hour from Mexico – map

        3. Where it is located – map

        4. John Zipperstein, *Tucson Magazine*

    B. Feel*ing* charmed by the unique Sonoran desert lifestyle

        1. Peaceful and relaxing – cacti

        2. Seeing beautiful mountain views – slides

        3. Being a part of the "Old West" – slides

        4. Great places to visit – slides

    C. Gett*ing* an inside look at the economy

        1. University of Arizona studies

        2. Chamber of Commerce – brochures

        3. Growth rate in population

        4. Why one lives there

III. Conclusion. Type: _Cool Quote_

☑Check this box if your claim is paraphrased and reinforced here.

Functions of the Persuasive Message Strategy

Let us look more closely at the three main parts of the Persuasive Message Strategy — the *introduction*, *body*, and *conclusion*.

The function of the introduction is to provide a highly dramatic way to get immediate and complete attention from your receivers. William James emphasized that until you have achieved your receivers' complete and undivided attention, then no other information can be effectively communicated in the rest of your speech.

The function of the body is to provide "interesting support " for your claim, usually in the form of three to five major points, A, B, C, D, and E. Interesting support is information that is: (1) highly interesting to your receivers and (2) highly supportive of your claim. You may have noticed that only three major points, A, B, and C, are shown in our sample Persuasive Message Strategy. If desired, you may add more major points. Under each major point, at least four minor points (1-4) are listed; you may also add more of these if you wish.

The function of the conclusion is to provide a dramatic and conclusive closing signal to your receivers so they will know your speech is finished.

As a general rule, the introduction and conclusion comprise no more than twenty percent of the total time of a speech. The goals of the introduction and conclusion are simple — to lead into or lead out of the body of the speech, respectively. Therefore, time spent on these parts needs to be brief.

Introductions and Conclusions

Which type of introduction and conclusion can you choose?

How about the one that is most interesting to your receivers because that will ensure more sharing and hence more communication. Remember those Venn diagrams from previous chapters?

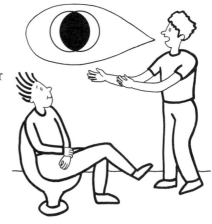

Here are nearly two dozen types of highly interesting introductions and conclusions. When you create your Persuasive Message Strategy, write the abbreviation of each type (listed below on the right hand side) as the verbal cue as what to say in your speech.

Introductions	Types
Arouse curiosity	*Mystery*
Relate a poignant personal story or one about someone else	*Poignant Story*
Tell a dramatic story as an example of your claim or major point	*Illustrative Story*

Introductions (cont.)	**Types**
Use a vivid demonstration	*Demonstration*
Ask a very interesting question	*Inquiry*
State a highly interesting quotation	*Cool Quote*
Show how your claim has a deep impact on your receivers	*Impact*
Present amazing facts	*Amazing Facts*
Propose something your receivers can gain by listening	*Purpose*
Create something to get your receivers' immediate and complete attention — create your own type of introduction	*Original*

The late Johnny Carson, the famous television entertainer, was reported to have quipped when asked about humor, that dying was easy — people do that naturally, but

 comedy is a whole other matter, and to succeed takes real effort! So, if one of America's funniest comedians believes humor is difficult to pull off — unless you are as skilled at comedy as a Jerry Seinfeld or Whoopi Goldberg — avoid the "funny" introduction.

Another introduction and conclusion that most receivers do not like is the "apology." Why? An apology puts the speaker in an unequal status to her receivers. An apology says, *I did something wrong.* Your receivers are more interested in hearing what you did right, or they would not have asked you to speak.

Conclusions	**Types**
Repeat or review your major points	*Summary*
Request some type of action	*Request*
Give your receivers a sincere note of appreciation	*Gratitude*
Quote a highly interesting verse of poetry or piece of literature	*Literary Art*
State a highly interesting and well-known quote	*Cool Quote*
State your most interesting major point; rise to an informational peak	*Clincher*
Get "up close and personal" with a challenge to accept or adopt your claim	*Challenge*
Say something humorous; by the end of your speech, your receivers will more likely get your punch lines	*Funny*
Create what would be an extremely dramatic and conclusive closing signal to your receivers — create your own type of conclusion	*Original*

Types of Persuasive Bodies

The final aspect to consider before you create your Persuasive Message Strategy is the type of "persuasive body." This is the pattern or organization of the three to five major points in the body of your speech.

All forms of communication, not just speeches, are organized according to an inductive or deductive type of persuasive body. All other types of persuasive bodies are a variation of these two types. So you are aware of these so-called "garden-varieties," they are also listed here. Nevertheless, it is highly recommended that you only use the inductive or deductive type of persuasive body.

The Two Primary Types of Persuasive Bodies

Inductive. Type of persuasive body in which all the interesting support leads up to or is presented before the claim statement. The claim is said for the first time in the conclusion of the Persuasive Message Strategy.

Deductive. Type of persuasive body in which the claim is presented in the introduction and followed by the rest of the interesting support in the remainder of the Persuasive Message Strategy. The claim may also be stated in the conclusion. However, in this case, it is merely a restatement, because the *cat was already let out of the bag* in the introduction.

Garden-Varieties of Persuasive Bodies

Time. Major points in the body of a speech are organized according to forward or reverse chronological order; the claim may be in the introduction or conclusion.

Space. Major points in the body of a speech are organized according to geographical or physical location; the claim may be in the introduction or conclusion.

Topical. Major points in the body of a speech are organized according to significant divisions, subjects, or areas of knowledge; the claim may be in the introduction or conclusion.

Comparison and Contrast. Major points in the body of a speech are organized according to their similarities and differences to other major points of conflicting claim statements; the claim may be in the introduction or conclusion.

Problem-Solution. Major points in the body of a speech are organized according to the presentation of one or more highly interesting problems. Each problem is followed by at least one highly interesting solution that will support the claim; the claim may be in the introduction or conclusion.

Least Important to Most Important, Most Familiar to Least Familiar, Simplest to Most Complex. Major points in the body of a speech are organized in ascending or descending order, depending on which one of these types is chosen; the claim may be in the introduction or conclusion.

Creating Your Persuasive Message Strategy

You are now ready to create your Persuasive Message Strategy.

Use the following step-by-step instructions to guide you as you complete a blank Persuasive Message Strategy in the Appendix.

Step 1: Ask yourself this essential question:

What facts, opinions, and experiences are my receivers highly interested in?

This is a reminder to consider all of the previous sections of the Communication Guide as you complete these steps.

Step 2: Write your claim on the top of your Persuasive Message Strategy next to the words Claim Statement.

Step 3: Denote, by check mark in the box provided, your choice of whether your claim will be stated in the introduction *or* conclusion. Note that the instructions on the Persuasive Message Strategy also say to *paraphrase* and *reinforce* your claim wherever you decide to say it.

Paraphrase means to say your claim in "different words that mean the same thing" so it is much more interesting to your receivers.

A speaker could say her claim almost exactly like it is written on the Persuasive Message Strategy; for example, she could say, *I want my receivers to primarily believe that eating at fast-food restaurants is healthy as a result of listening to my speech.* This statement is twenty-two words long. Does this sound interesting to you?

Instead, this speaker can paraphrase her claim as: *The main point of my speech is that eating at fast-food restaurants is healthy,* which is only fourteen words long (noticeably shorter in length). As you can see, the paraphrasing of her claim has made it much more concise, easier-to-understand, and easier-to-remember — much more interesting.

Reinforce means that when you state the paraphrased version of your claim, that it is "emphasized in some way." This helps gain even more of your receivers' attention on your claim.

Using the previous example, some of the possible techniques to reinforce the claim include writing it on the board in the front of the room, passing out small copies of the claim to each of the receivers, and repeating it orally two or three times in a row. You also may create unique methods to reinforce your claim, such as asking your receivers to sing your claim after you first state it.

Step 4: Denote, by check mark in the box provided, your choice to use either the inductive or deductive type of persuasive body.

Step 5: Denote, by using the abbreviated wording, the type of introduction and conclusion that you plan to use in your speech.

Step 6: Denote your interesting support, your major and minor supporting points, in the body of your Persuasive Message Strategy.

Denote the major points first, then add minor points underneath these major points. Before listing each point, ask yourself the question in Step 1.

A key part of this step is: The major points, A-E, come only from the Behaviors section in your Receiver Analysis. This is because experiences are the most persuasive type of information.

As for the minor points, 1-4, they come from any section of the Communication Guide, including other behaviors from your Receiver Analysis.

When you want to denote the use of a communication channel — a video, chart, or handout — remember to write a shortened version of the actual channel next to the point that will be explained or supported by using a hyphen (-).

Step 7: Review your completed Persuasive Message Strategy and make changes.

If you need additional interesting support because the body lacks a major or minor supporting point, first create new predictions in each of the previous four sections of your Communication Guide. Then, ask yourself the question in Step 1 and decide which additional prediction you wish to change to a new point.

When you are creating a prepared speech, this is the step in which you write the script. Write your script in an essay format using the Persuasive Message Strategy as a guide. Write at least one paragraph for the introduction, one paragraph for the conclusion, and one paragraph for each major point. Complete this script before going to the last step.

Step 8: Have fun practicing and then delivering your highly interesting speech!

What about Impromptu Speeches?

With this type of speech, a speaker does not have enough time to completely plan her speech. This is because the request for this speech is often unplanned, spontaneous, or "off-the-cuff." Nevertheless, the speaker's audience will not accept a lack of preparation time as a reason for a bad performance. What is the solution?

It is an easy-to-use *Abridged Communication Guide* — a type of memory aid to use for all your upcoming impromptu speeches. Here is how it works.

> First, the moment you are informed of your speech topic, think back to *your most memorable personal experience* that relates to the topic.

> Second, create a knowledge, attitudinal, or behavioral claim that is supported or proven by this personal experience.

> Third, begin speaking right after you decide to use either an inductive or deductive persuasive body to organize the location of your claim and personal experience within your impromptu speech.

The Abridged Communication Guide is highly effective because memorable personal experiences are a "deep well" of information. In other words, they contain a great amount of highly ingrained information — our most vivid *prerecorded* thoughts, feelings, and emotions — that are just waiting for us to use. When you recall such an experience for your impromptu speech, you gain instant access to this information. You also will discover that this type of personal experience is already very well organized. As a result, the preparation for your speech will be quick and efficient — exactly what you need for a successful impromptu speech.

Chapter 9
Using the Discussion Format

After the Applause, Then What?

After the conclusion of a speech, a speaker can use the *Discussion Format*. The Discussion Format will increase your skills in leading a discussion and provide you with important feedback regarding your speech.

You may ask your receivers to write their answers or respond orally. An advantage of written feedback is that responses can be made anonymously which increases their credibility. And, written feedback provides an easy way to study the responses after each speech or several speeches.

The key to achieving benefits from the Discussion Format is how you interpret your receivers' comments. Look for "trends" — the same comment coming from *more than half* of your receivers. Conclusions drawn from trends are highly reliable. For example, if two-thirds of your receivers tell you *Your chart was very colorful,* then that is a trend. In this case, the conclusion that you used a very colorful chart is probably true.

The most important question is the first one. It asks your receivers to identify your claim statement. Novice speakers will often say their claim one way, yet write it on the board or pass it out in another form. As you may imagine, this creates confusion for your listeners. An effective speaker's goal is that 100 percent of her receivers can write or say the verbatim version of her claim from her speech. If she receives anything less, a speaker can safely conclude that she did not get her claim across. Other information in her speech also may not be effectively communicated.

Discussion Format

The Discussion Format includes the method of receiving feedback called the "compliment sandwich" — two positive pieces of information surround just one negative piece of information. This pattern helps a speaker digest or receive any negative information in a more acceptable manner.

Any criticism or ridicule, also called "heckling," need not be addressed by a speaker, or she can use this rebuttal — *All right, fine. Now what would you suggest?*

On the next page is a Discussion Format that you may use for your upcoming speeches. If you like, you may remove a perforated copy from the Appendix.

Discussion Format

Start your discussion by saying:

First, could you please tell me what you think my claim is?

Then use the "compliment sandwich":

1. What is one thing about my speech that you liked?

2. In order to help me, could you please give me one suggestion regarding how I could improve my speech?

3. As before, what is another thing about my speech that you liked?

Conclude by saying:

And finally, do you have any other comments or questions regarding my speech?

After all responses, then say:

Thanks for your help!

Chapter 10
Eliminating Speech Anxiety

A Little Scared?

Have you ever felt any of these because of a speech?

sweaty palms, feeling on edge, dry mouth, butterflies in the stomach, nervousness, shaky legs, racing thoughts, lump in the throat, indigestion, heart pounding, shaky hands, nausea, nervous twitches, weakness, sweating, anticipation of misfortune, difficulty concentrating, coldness in the hands and feet

If so, you have experienced *speech anxiety* — or what used to be called stage fright.

Exactly What Is Speech Anxiety?

Speech anxiety is "the mild and transient adverse symptoms of fear (like those cited above) that are triggered by the prospect of a speech performance, the performance itself, or the result of a speech performance." These symptoms vary from person to person, come from low self-confidence or low self-esteem, and are experienced by all speakers.

Most speech anxiety does not last very long or interfere with a person's daily routine. However, if any speech anxiety symptoms persist or become severe, such as a "pounding heart" (physical symptom) or anticipation of misfortune (psychological symptom), then a health professional should be consulted.

Speech anxiety is the *single biggest obstacle to becoming an effective speaker* which is why this entire chapter is devoted to the subject. It also is an obstacle to maintaining good psychological health. Therefore, an effective speaker's goal should be the *total elimination of speech anxiety* which will benefit you as a speaker and as a psychologically healthy individual. Unless you like feeling sick, no reason exists to keep any amount of your speech anxiety.

You may be interested in knowing some of the famous television and movie stars who have experienced similar bouts of anxiety regarding their performances. They include actress Jennifer Aniston, actor Michael Douglas, and singer Whitney Houston. So rest assured, your speech anxiety may feel uncomfortable, but you are definitely not alone.

What Is the Cure?

First, you need to change your thinking to incorporate *gratitude-based communication* (discussed in Chapter 1). Then, the remainder of the remedy for speech anxiety is your choices regarding the following:

effective speech practice and
effective speech anxiety reduction techniques.

Effective Speech Practice

You have two choices of the major types of effective speech practice: *traditional* and *progressive.*

In traditional speech practice, a speaker practices a speech at least two times. When to stop practicing? For both types, always stop practicing just before you are tired. That way, you avoid becoming burned out on your speech. You can actually practice too much, and when you do, your speech will not be fun anymore. So be careful not to "over practice."

In general, the more realistic the traditional practice, the more effective it will be in reducing speech anxiety as well as producing an excellent speech. Ideally, traditional practice occurs in the same room as your actual presentation and includes as many of your real receivers as possible. For obvious reasons, this is not very likely. However, the main point is to practice in a social and physical environment that is as close as possible to the actual setting of your speech. Despite what you may have heard and because realism is so important to traditional speech practice, practicing in front of your dog or mirror is not advised.

As for the progressive type of practice, it exclusively involves the mind. What this means is that in some ways it is much easier than the traditional type of practice. For progressive speech practicing, you merely close your eyes and imagine yourself giving your entire speech perfectly — and without any speech anxiety. Throughout your imaginary speech or visualization, see yourself as clearly as possible and with as much detail as possible. Also, while you practice, try to feel or experience your speech as you are visualizing it in your mind. This strengthens your mind-body connection and resultant memory. As much as possible, believe that you are really delivering your speech, and it is flawless and fearless.

Another advantage of progressive practice is that it is much faster than traditional practice. Why? You may remember that a typical person can think over two and one-half times faster than she can talk. So, in the same amount of time that it would take to practice one traditional speech, you could visualize it in your head nearly three times. Therefore, progressive speech practice can be a great form of time management.

Furthermore, unlike traditional practice, you can do progressive practice anywhere — waiting in line, your bedroom, an office, the library — anywhere, so long as you can concentrate with very few interruptions. A notable exception, however, is doing this type while driving; it is not suggested for safety reasons.

And finally, to get the best results from the progressive type of practice, first master the traditional method. Then, when you visualize yourself doing something perfectly in your speech, you will have some excellent past experience to base your thoughts on.

Effective Speech Anxiety Reduction Techniques

Like choices? Then here are nearly forty techniques from which to choose to help you totally eliminate speech anxiety.

1. When you have dry mouth — the feeling of lack of any moisture in your mouth and difficulty swallowing — drink more water, or bring a glass of water to the podium. When you perspire heavily on your forehead, wipe it with a handkerchief or tissue. If you have an annoying cough, use a throat lozenge.

2. Before your speech, think about it as sharing ideas that you already truly and deeply know, believe, or experience. As a result, when you actually give your speech, you will feel more confident because you are *speaking from your heart, not your notes.*

3. There are many similarities between public speaking and daily conversation. In that sense, you have been practicing aspects of public speaking your entire life. When you can picture your speech as nothing more than an enlarged version of conversation — with many years of related practice — then it will not seem so frightening.

4. *Do! Don't stew!* This is a pithy saying to tell yourself in your self-talk. When you are worried about an upcoming speech, tell yourself this phrase. It will remind you to change whatever you are worried about into something positive, such as doing additional practices of your speech or making another visual/ sensory aid.

5. Somebody had previously persuaded you to know, believe, or do whatever your claim is. As you are preparing your speech, muster up the same enthusiasm that convinced you. This enthusiasm will help replace the feelings that are creating your speech anxiety.

6. The type of feeling of wanting to communicate your claim more than anything else in the world is called "conviction." The higher your level of conviction, the less speech anxiety you will feel. So increase your conviction about your claim, and many of your anxieties will disappear.

7. Effective public speaking is primarily a human relations skill. This means that how an audience responds to the quality of your Claim Statement, Receiver Analysis, Source Credibility Analysis, Channel Characteristics Analysis, and Persuasive Message Strategy is what matters the most. Therefore, the most important lens in speech communication is the human one, not the lens of a video camera.

   When most speakers review their videotaped speeches, they usually focus on how they look and the technical skills involved in their presentation.

These are often highly negative aspects, such as the amount of *ums, ahs,* and unusual gestures and physical movements.

So when reviewing one of your speeches, concentrate on the positive feedback from your live audience — this is the most helpful kind.

8. *The show must go on!* This wise saying, which you can use in your self-talk, is a reminder to not worry about errors that occur during your speech; just make your corrections and continue delivering your speech.

9. You can eliminate much of your speech anxiety by learning how to handle "dysfluencies," or filler words such as the dreaded um or ah.

   When you feel the urge to say one, just pause one or two seconds. This might feel like a long time, but it is really not. This pause will give your brain enough time to prepare for your next statement, instead of using one of these words.

   Another major reason for too many ums and ahs is lack of practice and lack of enthusiasm. By practicing claims that are more exciting to you, less dysfluencies will be needed. They will magically disappear.

10. Though hard to believe, according to speech communication experts, most symptoms of speech anxiety are not noticeable by receivers unless they are so extreme as to nearly debilitate the speaker.

    Even better news is that research reveals that if receivers do notice a few symptoms of speech anxiety, they will not significantly lower their evaluation of the speaker or her speech.

    In other words, even if you feel like everyone can see how scared you are, do not worry, the data is clear: Your audience probably cannot tell and, even if they can see that you are afraid, they probably do not care!

11. Before you speak, create a reasonable goal about how much change you want in your receivers. After your speech is over, you can compare the actual outcome with this goal. Your speech anxiety will lessen as you change your goal to come closer to the typical responses from your receivers.

12. *What you resist, persists.* What this idea means is that as far as any particular speech anxiety symptom goes, such as saying um, one of the best things to do is to simply leave it alone. Do not repeatedly think about or mentally dwell on any symptom that is bothering you. This, in itself, will help lower its severity.

13. Receivers who carefully listen to the content of your speech, in general, are too busy concentrating on your ideas than counting ums and ahs. When you encounter people who count dysfluencies, do not be afraid of their comments. These comments are usually not related to the quality of your speech, but to the quality of the receiver.

14. When you are not writing your Communication Guide, every once in a while,

think about your speech. By the time you sit down to finish the preparation for your speech, you will find that some of your fears will have already been resolved.

15. Making mistakes is normal, natural, and even expected. That is what tells receivers you are being real. Most people like this, and some of the most popular television shows also highlight these so-called "bloopers."

    Most receivers want you to successfully bounce back from a pratfall. If you do hear laughter after a mistake in your speech, it is probably not directed at you but at the accident itself. Therefore, because mistakes are inevitable, spending more time practicing comebacks instead of worrying about making errors is advisable.

16. You can feel more confident by getting physically ready before you begin speaking. Here is how: Slowly walk to the podium, pause a moment while there to gather your thoughts, take a deep breath, and with your mind focused on your first sentence, begin your speech. You also can feel more confident by practicing returning to your seat after the conclusion of your speech.

17. If you think bad things will happen during your speech, then they probably will. This kind of thinking and the results from it are called a "negative self-fulfilling prophecy." Since most speech disasters do not happen, why forecast them?

    Instead, create a "positive self-fulfilling prophecy." Before your speech, think only about the good aspects that will be a part of your speech. For example, think about the great visual/sensory aids in your speech or the exciting and dramatic conclusion you will be using. With this kind of gratitude-based thinking, you will have less speech anxiety, and your actual speech will turn out better.

18. All great speeches are autobiographical. In other words, in a great speech, all you are really doing is talking about yourself. Much of your speech anxiety will disappear when you remember that "being yourself" not only helps make a great speech, it is the *only* way to make one.

19. In thinking about how well you delivered your speech, consider the "subjective-objective paradox." No one can see herself objectively on the outside while she is also the subject on the inside, or internal perspective.

    Since your receivers have an objective view of your performance, this is another reason that their feedback is more reliable than your own. So, to lessen your speech anxiety after your speech, concentrate mostly on your audience's comments.

20. *Have fun!* Having this as a goal enhances every aspect of your speech preparation, speech, and speech evaluation. So even if something goes terribly wrong — which it likely will not — at the very least, you had fun. Indeed, fun is one of the greatest antidotes for speech anxiety or any anxiety, for that matter.

21. Eye contact with the audience helps a speaker feel much more confident. The more eye contact you have in a speech, the more confident you will feel.

    To help increase eye contact with your receivers, look for "interested eyes." As you speak, look at the *eyes of your receivers who are looking back at you with interest* — concentrate on these receivers. Attempt to pick out even more of these kinds of eyes until you can look at all your receivers. Despite what you may have heard, imagining your receivers as naked, looking at a spot in the back of the room, and staring at the foreheads of your audience, are not as effective in gaining your receivers' attention as genuine eye-to-eye contact.

22. And speaking of eyes, James Cagney, the famous movie actor who earned a Lifetime Achievement Oscar for many outstanding movie performances, had a similar recommendation on eye contact. His advice was to step right up to your audience, look directly into their eyes, then tell them the truth of your presentation. This is another way of advising you to speak from your heart and not from your notes.

23. Having a *fit of fear?* Then, replace it with a *fit of courage!* This quote from William James explains how:

    Action seems to follow feeling, but really action and feeling go together; and by regulating the action, which is under the more direct control of the will, we can indirectly regulate the feeling, which is not.

    Thus, the sovereign voluntary path to cheerfulness, if our spontaneous cheerfulness be lost, is to sit up cheerfully and to act and speak as if cheerfulness were already there. If such conduct does not make you feel cheerful, then nothing else can.

    Therefore, to feel brave (feel high self-confidence), act as if we were brave (act as if we possessed high self-confidence), use all of our will to that end, and a courage-fit (intense feeling of self-confidence) will very likely replace the fit of fear (high speech anxiety).

24. An excellent method to create an overall feeling of relaxation is to visualize the most peaceful and serene natural environment that you have ever experienced — without any people in it — for a minimum of five minutes. Do  this at least ten minutes before your speech and immediately after your speech to alleviate speech anxiety symptoms.

    The process of visualization also can be used to overcome specific speech anxiety symptoms. For example, if you have "the butterflies," you can visualize setting them free. If you visualize them flying in formation, this is not enough, for the butterflies will still be around. They need to  be *totally* set free, because the goal is the *total* elimination of speech anxiety.

25. Exercising the day of your speech, shortly before your speech, and immediately

after your speech can be a great anxiety reducer. Since an effective exercise routine varies greatly from person to person, it is best to check with an exercise specialist to learn which exercises will work best for you.

26. You can get significant relief from common physical symptoms of speech anxiety such as headache, upset stomach, and indigestion from over-the-counter medications. If properly attended to, these symptoms can be totally eliminated. However, before you take any type of medication, check with your physician.

27. Do not worry about what you cannot control — how your receivers will respond to your speech. Instead, concentrate on what you can control — your speech preparation and delivery. In other words, do not waste your mental energy on things that cannot be changed.

28. Remember that your Persuasive Message Strategy is like a road map, there for you to refer to when you need it. You can feel more relaxed when you realize that you can always fall back on it if you get lost in your speech.

29. After each practice, "self-evaluate" your performance using your teacher's speech evaluation. If done correctly, you will know very specifically how well you are doing, thus increasing your self-confidence and self-esteem by reducing your anxiety about your grade for your upcoming speech.

30. Create a *Limit anxiety!* rule on how much speech anxiety you will allow yourself. Set a self-imposed limit on the amount of anxiety you will let build up within yourself, and when you reach it, simply stop the additional unwanted anxiety by firmly telling yourself, in your self-talk, to *Limit anxiety!* You will find, perhaps to your surprise, that this technique works because research shows that you will respond to your self-talk.

31. Here is another self-talk technique. Give yourself a dose of positive self-talk — a "self pep-talk" — before, during, or after speaking. For example, as you are delivering a speech, you can tell yourself supportive statements such as *Keep it up, you're doing great!* or *My demonstration is going just like I planned.* And, at the end of your speech, if speech anxiety persists, you can tell yourself, *Nice going, my chart really caught the audience's attention* or *Gee, my voice sounded very clear through the microphone.*

32. Rehearse the first sentence more than any other in your speech. This helps you feel more assured of getting off to a good start because you are more confident of the first words that you will say. If you need even more confidence getting started, rehearse your entire introduction more than any other part of the speech.

33. Alcoholic beverages and psychotropic (mind altering) drugs may reduce a small amount of speech anxiety, but their side effects significantly interfere with and reduce the quality of your speech. Therefore, the net gain from using such

substances is minimal, and it is recommended that you completely avoid them as speechmaking aids.

34. Whenever you experience speech anxiety, the quickest remedy is to slowly and gently inhale and exhale deep breaths of air. Nearly every relaxation technique involves this kind of deep breathing because it is so highly effective in reducing anxiety and stress.

35. Just plain scared of people? Then, "make friends" with your audience. Before getting up to speak, chat briefly with some of the people in the audience. You might introduce yourself, discuss an element of your speech, share a comment about a previous speaker, or talk about the weather. These short conversations create a kind of "warm-up," which can help you feel less anxious.

    If you still have speech anxiety after your speech, then you can create a "cool-down" experience with your audience. For example, you could talk with one of your receivers about something that you said in your speech, ask for a question about a handout that you gave, discuss what an audience member thought of how your voice sounded, or introduce yourself to additional audience members to help you feel more relaxed.

36. If you have *severe* speech anxiety — the type in which the symptoms are so extreme that they prevent you from speaking to any audience, do not lose hope.

    Highly successful therapies exist that can treat your condition. For more information, consult with a behavioral health expert in your area.

And Finally

Mike Ditka, the famous Football Hall of Fame coach and player, when asked what the goal for each of his teams was every season always had the same response: to win the Super Bowl.

No matter how talented his teams were, no matter what their previous record was, no matter how many injuries they had sustained, Coach Ditka never changed this goal — to achieve the absolute pinnacle of success. When asked why he had such an ideal goal, his philosophy was quite simple; he believed that having perfection as a goal would always increase the quality of his team's performance and outcome, regardless of their ability.

When translated as advice regarding speech anxiety, this means that no matter how many symptoms you may have, you should always aim for the highest goal: *the total elimination of speech anxiety.*

Chapter 11
Freeing Yourself from Microphone Fears

Karaoke to Computers

From small children playing karaoke to business people video conferencing, microphones are nearly everywhere. To be fully prepared for a speech, you need to consider that a microphone may be a part of your speaking environment, even if it is only for recording purposes.

Some speakers experience what is called *mic fright,* or the fear of using a microphone. This chapter explains how to effectively use a microphone.

Tips and Suggestions

> Using a microphone does not need to profoundly change the way in which you deliver your speech, such as your inflection and tone of voice. The most important adjustment in your delivery is the rate of your speech, slowed slightly to compensate for the echo of the microphone.

> Most microphones used for speeches are unidirectional. They hear or pick up your voice from one spot only, usually the very top, or the "head" of the microphone. Make sure you know exactly where that spot is on the microphone and speak directly into that area.

> Before you begin to speak, move the microphone to accommodate your posture. For example, raise the head of the microphone to avoid bending when you speak. And, before saying your first word, pause one second to double-check that you are ready to begin speaking.

> Check for an "on-off" switch slightly below the head of the microphone. After you have completed all the physical adjustments of the microphone, move this switch to the "on" position. (If the microphone is left on and the audience hears the noise from your adjustments, then they will probably expect you to begin your speech.)

If no such switch exists, and you do not know if the microphone is on, the best way to check is to tap lightly on the head of the microphone several times. This method will usually not attract the audience's attention. If you talk into the microphone or blow on it, you will probably get your receivers' attention, but this will occur before you are ready to start speaking.

> Speak between six to twelve inches from the microphone. Say your first sentences slowly so as to gauge the volume of your amplified voice.

You might be too loud (too close to the microphone) or too soft (too far from the microphone). If so, adjustments are needed. For example, if your voice is too soft, you may: slowly move your face and body closer to the microphone, slowly raise the volume control of the microphone, or move the microphone to a position that is closer to your mouth (the latter should be tried last since it is the most distracting). Reverse these procedures if you are too loud for your audience.

> A common cause of microphone feedback, a high-pitched squealing sound, is the placement of the hand over the head of the microphone. Because of the annoying sound this action creates, you will want to avoid this at all times.

> If you have the opportunity, practice with the microphone beforehand. Perform some of the small but highly noticeable things that you may do near the microphone during your speech, such as turning pages in a book. Never chew, eat, or drink anything within the unidirectional zone of a microphone; when amplified, these sounds are highly distracting and annoying.

> Remember to breathe naturally while speaking through a microphone. Sometimes speakers forget to do this, which makes giving a speech with a microphone a "breathtaking" experience.

> If your receivers laugh or give you similar audible responses, make sure to wait until their reactions have subsided. Otherwise, the sound of their responses will drown out or interfere with the next words that you say through the microphone.

> Some words have strong "popping" consonants like "p" or "b." Most microphones have built-in devices to handle this problem. As such, do not change how you say these words or how closely you speak to the microphone.

> Concentrate on communicating, not on the sound of your voice through the microphone. Because of the slight delay of your voice echoing back to you, you can become distracted if you try to talk and hear yourself at the same time. Simply speak into the microphone and enjoy how strong and powerful you sound.

Chapter 12
Mastering the Art of Conversation

Only Two

The type of speech communication that involves only two people, or one person talking with another person, is called *dyadic communication*. The two individuals are referred to as a "dyad."

In this chapter, the most current concepts of dyadic communication — nicknamed the *art of conversation* — are presented. These concepts will help you prepare for one of the most important conversations in your life, the employment interview, which is discussed in the next chapter.

Turn-Taking

When a dyad member switches from being a source to a receiver, a speaking "turn" has occurred. "Turn-taking" is the term that describes this process in a conversation.

The more equal in status the source in a dyad considers her receiver, the more the source will share equally: (1) the number of times she speaks and (2) the length of time she speaks.

An example of this is a factory supervisor talking with a line worker. The supervisor, with greater status than her employee, usually has more speaking turns as well as more time to speak. A possible exception is a highly respected worker; she usually has more speaking turns and more speaking time than other such employees.

Topic Management

Dyad members talk about topics that relate to their needs. When the needs of one dyad member change during a conversation, this change leads to new topics. If both members do not switch to the new topic or topics, then two separate monologues result. In this case, both dyad members are hearing each other, but neither is really listening to or comprehending the other. Perhaps you have experienced this before; it has been facetiously called the "sounds of silence."

For example, imagine two friends having lunch together; one is interested in talking about her argument with her husband; the other, her problem with her new boss. As the conversation progresses, no single topic emerges as the common one of the dialogue. Instead, each dyad member talks only about her particular topic — either the spousal problem or the job problem. As a result, despite all the words uttered and voices heard, there really is no communication or sharing of ideas.

The Major Parts of a Dyadic Conversation

The dialogue that occurs between dyad members which composes the first turn-taking sequence within a conversation is called the "introduction."

As dyad members respond to each other with more dialogue via additional turn-taking, then they create the "body," or middle part of a conversation.

The dialogue that makes up the final turn-taking sequence between the participants is called the "conclusion."

For example, the common expression *What's going on?* is the first turn of a person who is eager to begin a conversation. When another person responds, *Not too much, what's going on with you?*, then this initial turn-taking sequence has become the introduction of their conversation.

As more talk is exchanged, the amount of each member's skill at creating and managing interesting topics will determine the depth and length of the body of the conversation.

Finally, one dyad member will tell the other dyad member that she is ready to end the conversation. Statements such as, *Well, I really need to get back to the office* or *I hope you don't mind, but I've got some homework, can we talk later?* are communicated. If the other dyad member, in her turn to speak, responds by agreeing to the proposed termination, then the conversation has created its conclusion.

Speaking Compared to Thinking

According to the latest research, the typical speaking rate of a person is 150 to 200 words per minute. Although this may seem fast, the experts also have found that the average person can think much faster — up to 600 words per minute.

Therefore, in a typical dyadic conversation, while one person is talking, the other person may be thinking about something else or planning what to say next. An effective source knows this and chooses topics that are highly interesting to a receiver. Good listeners or receivers, in their spare "brain time," are usually hard at work connecting what the other dyad member is saying to what they already know.

For example, one member of a dyad is recommending a new restaurant by describing its location, menu, and prices. A good listener would be thinking about these aspects as they relate to her, such as how many minutes the restaurant is from her home and how much it would cost to bring her family to dine. When a topic is uninteresting, a good listener still is thinking about what the source is saying. In this case, she might think about how to create an appropriate verbal transition to another topic of greater interest to both dyad members.

Norm of Reciprocity

The "norm of reciprocity" means that a receiver in a dyad will automatically, in most situations, respond the same way in which the source sends a message. Essentially, this is an "interpersonal reflex" in the sense that it happens so fast that a receiver will rarely think about her quick and natural response that is so similar to what was originally sent.

For example, a teacher may speak to a student in a hostile way with an accusing tone of voice when she says, *Where's your homework?* As a result, the teacher is very likely to hear an equally hostile response from the student: *Where do you think it is?*

Here is another example that relates to the concept of source credibility. It pertains to the saying, *Until a person knows you care, that person doesn't care how much you know.*

By applying the norm of reciprocity, this saying means that if your goal is to achieve a positive and caring response regarding your ideas from a receiver (to achieve high trustworthiness source credibility), then you need to be the first person in the dyad to communicate in a positive and caring way.

Meaning Is in People — Not Words

The source of the words that dyad members use are either denotative (come from a dictionary) or connotative (come from common usage). With both types, the meaning is based on how each member decodes or interprets each word. Likewise, nonverbal communication, or as it is commonly called, "body language," is also understood differently by each dyad member.

Therefore, dyadic communication is a type of symbolic communication, and it is based on a person's interpretation of symbols: words (verbal communication) and body language (nonverbal communication).

An example of this is when someone first greets you and says, with a smile and hand wave, *How are you doing?* At the denotative level, you could conceivably respond with your latest medical report. Because you do not typically interpret this as your receiver's desired response, you will likely respond based on a commonly known type of connotative meaning that creates an orderly flow of conversation such as *Fine, how are you?*

Perception Is Reality

Dyad members base their responses on what they *perceive* the other dyad member is saying.

Think about the previous example of greeting another person. Even though the initial question inquired about the general status of the receiver, the most likely response is based on what the receiver perceives that the source wanted to hear. In this case, the most likely perception is that the source merely wanted a short response to signal the start of the dialogue such as *Not too bad, how are you doing?*

Dyadic Communication Is Equivocal

Because there is a high likelihood of variation in responses by a receiver, the process of dyadic communication involves a great amount of uncertainty.

At present, the belief that a dyad member has the ability to perfectly communicate any information is considered erroneous by speech communication experts; nevertheless, individuals should continue to strive for perfect communication.

Microgestures

Microgestures are extremely small, lightning quick kinds of body language that are hidden from another communicator. They are small chinks in the armor of a dyad member, which make them highly reliable indicators of a dyad member's deeper feelings.

For example, imagine an interviewer who offers you a cup of coffee as the interview begins. To determine how genuine the offer is, you can confirm or deny your curiosity by detecting a microgesture. Let us say the interviewer goes down the hall to get you this cup of coffee and brings it back to the office. Before taking a seat, the interviewer sets the coffee in front of you. In this situation, what microgesture could you detect?

At this point, you would be expected to pick up the coffee and take a drink. Instead, because you are familiar with microgestures, you could look for the hidden body language of the interviewer.

Indeed, you find one microgesture. While the interviewer was getting settled in a chair about to begin the interview, you notice a brief, perhaps a half-second, look of strain on the interviewer's face. For this fraction of a second, the interviewer's facial expression reminded you of a weight lifter who had just tried to lift too many pounds. Hmm, what does this mean?

This microgesture — the grimace — seems to contradict the polite offer by the interviewer to get coffee. With this new knowledge gained from this microgesture, it may be reasonable to conclude that your interviewer's courtesy does not come easy. It may now appear that the interviewer was expending extra energy to get your coffee as a means of impressing you.

Stimulus Discrimination Versus Stimulus Generalization

This does not mean that being prejudiced against someone increases communication effectiveness: It means something much different. Stimulus discrimination is the psychological process that dyad members use to determine how each member is *different* from each other. Stimulus discrimination strives toward making predictions about the individuality of each dyad member. The result of this type of psychological analysis is messages within the dialogue that focus on the differences of each dyad member.

Compare this to the opposite process, stimulus generalization, in which dyad members determine how each member is *similar* to each other. In this case, predictions are made as a way to determine how members in a dyad are *alike*. Therefore, dyadic communication based on stimulus generalization focuses on how dyad members are the same.

So, to be an effective dyad member, *be aware of which process* — stimulus discrimination or stimulus generalization — that is being used in your dyadic communication.

Nonverbal Communication and Credibility

Communication research has revealed that in dyadic communication the words that each member uses are not as credible as the nonverbal or physical behavior that goes along with it.

For example, one member of a dyad says to the other member that she would like to meet later to see a movie. If the receiver of this message has her arms folded, is standing three or more feet away, and has low eye contact — and even if this member verbally expresses interest in the offer — it is much more likely that, at some point, the offer will be rejected (as indicated by the defensive body language).

The Most Interesting Nonverbal Behaviors

Within a dialogue, the most interesting nonverbal behaviors are a *smile* and *sincere eye contact*.

Communication research has determined that these are part of a universal set of nonverbal behaviors; they are understood within all cultures. Nevertheless, the specific type, duration, and amount that are interesting still requires the use of stimulus discrimination. In other words, the exact kind of smile and sincere eye contact that you may choose within a conversation are based on your predictions regarding your receiver.

As for an employment interview — one of the most important conversations that you will ever have — a smile and sincere eye contact are absolutely essential for success. This is something to keep in mind as you read the next chapter.

Nearly Everyone Loves a Great Listener

If you remember this, you will have better conversations and more friendships as a result of learning how to listen more effectively to other people.

What is the easiest way to become a more effective listener?

Just sincerely care about the people that you talk with and ask lots of questions. Questions invite people to speak, and when your questions are interesting, you will get very natural responses and become interesting to other people.

There is one other thing to mention regarding the effective use of questions. Because most people do not like to be told what to do, the use of questions instead of direct orders or commands will help you get more positive responses from other people.

Never Criticize Anyone for Any Reason

The single most destructive type of dyadic communication is the type that attacks a dyad member, or criticism.

The most significant kinds of criticism include put-downs, name-calling, threats, obscenity, interference, mean shouting, and mean joking (examples cited in Chapter 1). The less these exist in a dyad, the more successful the dyadic communication will be. So, avoid criticizing anyone for any reason.

Chapter 13
Interviewing for Success

Achieving Success

A career position may be worth well over a million dollars — the amount that a typical employee earns in thirty years. And, this projection does not even account for inflation or include benefits such as health insurance. As a potential employee, you will need an "employment agreement," or an acceptance of a job offer, to be hired for such a position.

What is the single most important step in achieving this success?

It is the employment interview:

The goal of the employment interviewing process, which is composed of one or more interviews, is an employment agreement.

Within an employment interview, the two most important traits of the members are their "chemistry" and communication skills. Unfortunately, no book has the power to change a person's chemistry, or the biochemical makeup that a person was born with. On the other hand, an individual's communication skills can be upgraded.

According to employment specialists, the best candidate for a job usually does not get hired; instead, the applicant who *appears* to be the best candidate is usually hired. In other words,

The qualifications that an applicant possesses are not as important as the communication skills that are used to talk about these qualifications.

This amazing revelation leads to the purpose of this chapter: to help you significantly improve your interviewing communication skills — the key to interviewing for success.

Getting Started

Remember the adage, *Speaking without thinking is like shooting a gun without aiming.* Because interviewing is a type of speech communication, this idea also pertains to employment interviewing. You need to effectively and carefully plan your interview in advance in order to hit your target.

In contrast to giving speeches, however, there are some major changes in the interview preparation process. Instead of using the entire Communication Guide, only the Persuasive Message Strategy is necessary — with some modifications. And, as a means of practicing, you can conduct a role-playing game in which one person is the interviewer and one person is the interviewee. This training method, also called "simulation," is the best way to increase your communication skills in an interview.

Dyadic Introductions and Conclusions

In beginning your preparation for an employment interview, here is a list of the special types of dyadic introductions and conclusions that can be used in the Persuasive Message Strategy.

The purpose of the introduction is to create a highly interesting first impression, and the purpose of the conclusion is to produce a highly interesting last impression.

Introductions	Conclusions
Small Talk. A friendly but short mention of current events — the latest news, weather, sports.	*Small Talk.* (Same as introductions)
Gratitude. An appreciative traditional greeting or farewell: *Thank-you, I'm glad to hear, Good luck to you.*	*Gratitude.* (Same as introductions)
Reminder. A reinforcement of a previous idea: *I remembered to bring my work samples, As I said, I'm the hardest worker.*	*Reminder.* (Same as introductions)
Bold. A cheerful, sincere exclamation: *This place is beautiful!, What a gorgeous office!*	*Response.* A request of your receiver to do something: *Could you please send me another application?*
Original. A totally unique and memorable way to start the dialogue — your own type of dyadic introduction.	*Original.* A very clever way to end the dialogue — your own type of dyadic conclusion.

As part of every introduction and conclusion, always include a firm, entire hand, one to two second handshake. And, while shaking the interviewer's hand, always use direct eye contact the entire time.

After you conclude an interview, within five business days, send your interviewer a brief thank-you note or thank-you e-mail expressing your appreciation for the interview. If you predict that your interviewer wants additional information about your qualifications, include that in your correspondence as well.

By the way, there are no special types of bodies that are used in the Persuasive Message Strategy. Therefore, choose either the inductive or deductive type, just as you do when you prepare your speeches. The primary function of those types is to support your claim statement made in either the introduction or conclusion.

Dress

You may have heard the expression *You never get a second chance to make a first impression.* When you apply this to the employment interview, you must carefully choose the right dress — the clothing and the accompanying jewelry, hairstyle, and makeup — for your interview.

Because of the diversity of jobs and the more casual style of clothing in today's workforce, it is difficult to make generalizations regarding what to wear. Dress is part of a company's "corporate culture," the organization's internal, and often unwritten, rules. Therefore, to dress appropriately, you need to learn the company's "dress code" before your interview.

You may want to visit the company or talk to a current employee to learn the best dress for your interview. In general, dress similarly to the company's employees who are already doing the job you want. In other words, in your interview, your goal is to "look the part" of an employee who is already hired. By doing this, you are making it easier for the interviewer to visualize you in the job. And, if you are applying for a new position at the company, dress the way you predict that the interviewer would like to see you attired.

On a related note, if you role-play the interviewer, you also need to conform to the specific dress code for the company that you are representing.

For more specific ideas on what the proper business and professional dress is, either for men or women, "clothing engineer" John Molloy has an outstanding series of books on the subject.

Sample Interviewer Questions

The next two sections contain typical questions and *tough questions* that you will encounter as an interviewee. You will experience many of them as a part of nearly every interview.

If you thoroughly practice answering these questions and other questions like them, then you will feel confident that you can effectively answer *any question from any interviewer.*

If you role-play the interviewer, then the following will provide you with some great questions to ask.

1. *Why did you apply to our company?*

2. *Would you tell me about yourself?*

3. *Where do you expect to be in one year, three years, five years?*

4. *How would you rate yourself as a candidate?*

5. *What is your greatest strength and greatest weakness?*

6. *Can you give me an example of how you faced a major problem and solved it?*

7. *Why did you leave your last job?*

8. *How do you handle stress?*

9. *How would you describe your ideal boss and ideal job?*

10. *What motivates you to do the type of work required for this job?*

11. *What is your philosophy of management (or related topic)?*

12. *What does teamwork mean to you?*

13. *What salary are you interested in earning?*

14. *Why should we consider you compared to all other applicants?*

15. *How do you define success at both the business and personal levels?*

If you are asked about "references" either by an interviewer or as part of the employment application, here is an important tip. The individuals that you state or list need to be the ones with the highest source credibility because they are the most persuasive. For example, if you have the choice of citing a "department manager" or a "sales representative" as a work reference, the department manager is usually the best choice. Using this same example, if you only have sales representatives from which to choose, the best choice would still be the person with the highest source credibility — the one that you predict the interviewer would see as possessing the most education, experience, and work accomplishments.

Those Tough Questions

How do you handle questions from interviewers that seem virtually impossible to answer — the so-called "tough questions"?

Here are a couple of examples.

"Hypothetical questions," or questions about imaginary, highly difficult work-related problems, are often tough questions. These questions include highly technical questions, such as *How would you compute the exact depth that is needed for Mr. Parizo's custom pool?* Or, you may be asked a very tricky ethical question, such as *What would you do if you caught your secretary stealing from the petty cash fund?* And, although the time may be limited, you may even be asked to demonstrate a specific skill; for example, you may be asked a hypothetical question like *Could you please create a design or graphic that you might use for our local shoe company's ad campaign?*

"Inkblot questions," or questions that are covert psychological tests, are another one of the common types of tough questions. These ask you to compare yourself to animals, plants, or colors. Here are some typical inkblot questions: *Of all the animals, which one is most like you and why?* and *What color do you like most and hate most and why?*

The best way to answer tough questions is to *be prepared to be unprepared.* In other words, plan to answer tough questions with responses that will give you more time to prepare your final answer to the question. If you use the extra time, you are much more likely to give an excellent answer to the interviewer.

Here are some easy-to-remember responses that will help you be prepared to be unprepared:

That is a good question. May I have a moment to think about my answer?

Frankly, I don't know the answer to that question right now.
(This may actually be the answer the interviewer wants.)

I'm going to need a little time to think about that question.
Can we come back to it in a few minutes?

Could you please explain what you mean by that question?
I need a little more information to give you my answer.

Sample Interviewee Questions

As the interviewee, you may want to ask some of these very interesting questions of your interviewer.

Of course, if you role-play the interviewer, then you will need to be prepared to hear the following questions.

1. *Based on my application and resume, what in it interested you enough to call me for an interview?*

2. *What are the opportunities for promotion within the company?*

3. *Is there anything else, such as my college business classes, that I can tell you about myself?*

4. *How do you like working for your company?*

5. *Does your company belong to the Chamber of Commerce or other trade or service organizations?*

6. *Is there any on-the-job training required or given after I am hired?*

7. *Where is the person who previously held this position?*

8. *May I send you additional information about my qualifications?*

9. *How often will I be evaluated, by whom, and through what type of evaluation process?*

10. *What are a typical day, week, and year like for the person in this position?*

11. *Could you tell me more about your company's . . . ?*

12. *I have a specific question regarding your company's health benefits. What if . . . ?*

13. *How many applicants for this position do you have?*

14. *How long have you been seeking a person for this position?*

15. *If I am selected to be interviewed again, what should I expect from the next interview?*

K.I.S.S. or Not?

This question is not about whether you need to kiss your interviewer or interviewee, but about how to "Keep It Short and Simple." In other words, during each person's speaking turn in an interview, should your answers or questions be short, long, or in-between?

As a general rule:

> *The amount of talking during each person's speaking turn in an interview is determined by doing a receiver analysis of the interviewer or interviewee.*

Before you begin each speaking turn in an interview, you can predict the amount of talking that the other person wants as either a response to a question or as a question. Your predictions may vary from as short as one word to as long as several minutes — *it all depends on your receiver.*

The most effective way to make these predictions is to ask yourself, in your self-talk, *How long an answer or question does my receiver want?* If this does not produce a useful prediction, instead of just guessing, which is likely to result in the wrong amount of talking, you may politely ask the other person, *Would you like more information about my question or answer?*

Illegal Questions, Illegal Actions

Federal law prohibits employers from selecting employees on the basis of race, color, religion, sex, national origin, marital status, disability, or age. Areas related to these major demographics also are covered.

To avoid litigation, some employers include specialists in employment law to serve as monitors during interviews. These monitors protect the company by ensuring that all employment laws, at both the state and federal levels, are adhered to. They also help applicants by fostering a fair and equitable interviewing process.

"Illegal questions" are those sometimes-asked questions that violate employment law. And because these questions are illegal, your answers to these questions also are illegal. As soon as you answer this type of question and your answer is recorded as part of your application, the company is legally required to eliminate you as an applicant.

What happens if an employer continues to consider you after having recorded an illegal response? In this case, the employer is clearly acting outside the law. If discovered, the employer will face serious legal consequences and, at some future time, you also may lose your job with this company.

The best response to an illegal question is to politely decline to answer. And, the choice to explain to the interviewer that the question is illegal is left to your discretion. Keep in mind that any company that does not follow the law is probably not the company for you.

To find out more about illegal questions or illegal actions of potential employers, check with your school's career services department, state employment office, or district federal employment office. The U.S. Equal Employment Opportunity Commission, or EEOC, is the official agency that enforces all federal laws. You may learn more about the EEOC by researching their web site at http://www.eeoc.gov.

Money and More

After all the major issues between the applicant and employer have been discussed and agreed upon, the *salary and benefits negotiation* within an interview usually begins. This is the process in which the applicant and employer discuss the wages and incentives that the employer will offer the applicant.

The interviewer starts the negotiation by making the "initial offer." The interviewee's polite rejection of this offer begins the negotiation. However, if the initial offer is not rejected, then the next step by the employer is the offer to hire the applicant, which results in an employment agreement.

For an interviewee to successfully negotiate for a higher salary and benefits, she needs to supply interesting reasons to the interviewer that will motivate her to change the initial offer. The most interesting reasons are the applicant's credentials and work experiences that support the desired increase. Another highly interesting and persuasive reason is the applicant's willingness to do additional job responsibilities in exchange for greater compensation.

How can you determine the exact amount of money and benefits to negotiate for — your "negotiation goal"?

First, you need to learn what most people already working at the prospective job are earning (excellent places to check were mentioned in the preceding section). Then, based on this information, you predict, as specifically as possible in regard to both salary and benefits, what you are worth as an employee in this job. The result is your

negotiation goal. Your negotiation will conclude when: (1) the employer agrees to your negotiation goal, (2) you accept the employer's lesser offer, or (3) you reject the position entirely.

Example

An applicant is interviewing for an open position as a graphic designer at a major toy manufacturer. The job was advertised as paying $60,000 per year plus full medical health insurance. The employer's minimum desired qualifications are a Bachelor's degree in graphic design or a related field and five years' related work experience. The applicant has reached the final interview with the manager of the art department, and the manager has just made the initial offer for the exact amount that was advertised.

The interviewee possesses a Bachelor's degree in graphic design and ten years' work experience as a graphic designer. She has researched the salary rates and benefits in her field. She predicts that most people working at positions similar to her prospective job earn from $65,000 to $80,000 per year and have full medical coverage.

After thinking it over, she decides that her negotiation goal is $70,000 per year with major medical coverage.

The applicant responds to the interviewer's initial offer by politely saying that she has twice the amount of the desired qualifications in years of work experience and, as a result, will accept the position for $72,000 per year and full medical coverage.

As you can imagine, the interviewer mulls the applicant's "counter-offer" over. She responds by offering the interviewee $66,000 per year with major medical coverage.

The interviewee takes a moment to think about this new offer and notes that $66,000 per year is higher than the initial offer of $60,000, and major medical coverage (which she definitely wants) is still part of the negotiation. Since not too many changes can be made in these two elements — including going back to the original offer — the negotiation is likely to conclude very soon. The interviewee thinks about her present state of good health and her rare use of her current medical coverage. She also thinks about her plan to buy a new house.

She decides to base her new response only on salary. She tells the interviewer that she will agree to the major medical coverage, but she desires $70,000 per year in salary. The interviewer pauses for a moment and then agrees to the interviewee's new salary goal. This salary and benefits negotiation has concluded, and the job offer is promptly made and accepted by the interviewee. An employment agreement has been successfully reached!

Could this negotiation have gone sour? Definitely. As you were reading this scenario, perhaps you may have thought of many other alternatives that could have occurred.

Honing Your Skills

Do you feel confident about your negotiating skills?

   If not, here is a fun and risk-free way to help you upgrade your skills. Go to several flea markets or garage sales and negotiate the price for a half-dozen items. Since bargaining is very common as well as expected in these very casual and informal environments, you can practice without fear of failure or embarrassment. The worst thing that could happen is that you could lose a negotiation for a secondhand item, which is nothing compared to losing an employer's offer for a first-rate career position.

The Last Preparation Step: Persuasive Message Strategy

To complete your Persuasive Message Strategy, either as an interviewer or interviewee, use the same steps that are listed in Chapter 8 (for speeches). The major differences are what have been presented in this chapter and the following key points.

   In an employment interview, unlike a speech, you probably will not have an overhead or chalkboard to help you reinforce your claim. Therefore, you reinforce it: (1) by using good eye contact, looking directly at your receiver or receivers as you state your claim and (2) by effectively using proxemics, remaining seated as you state your claim instead of rising or moving toward the door or exit. As for paraphrasing your claim, you do this in the same way as your speeches.

   In regard to the content of your major points and claim statements, they are shown on the next two pages as part of the recommended Persuasive Message Strategies for both the interviewer and interviewee. The Appendix contains additional copies, which you may remove for use in either a real interview or role-playing game.

   If desired, you may list supporting points 1, 2, 3, and 4, or you may omit them. You might also notice that the claims listed on the suggested Persuasive Message Strategies are for an *initial employment interview*. If you want, you may change these to better suit your actual interview.

   And finally, as an alternative to using a role-playing game as a means to prepare for an employment interview, you can use progressive practice, described in Chapter 10 on speech anxiety. The key advantage of using progressive practice for an employment interview is that you do not need another person; all you need to do is to visualize yourself perfectly communicating your Persuasive Message Strategy.

Interviewer Persuasive Message Strategy

Claim Statement: I want my interviewee to primarily *agree to prove that she is the most qualified applicant* as a result of our employment interview.

I. Introduction. Type:_____ (from dyadic list)

☐ Check this box; your claim is *paraphrased* and *reinforced* here.

II. Body. Check this box: ☐ Deductive

Please note: Supporting points 1-4 under A-D (below) may be omitted.

   A. *Learning about the job and company*

      1.

      2.

      3.

      4.

   B. *Being asked questions about qualifications*

      1.

      2.

      3.

      4.

   C. *Asking me questions*

      1.

      2.

      3.

      4.

   D. *Discussing areas of personal interest (spontaneous digressions/diversions)*

      1.

      2.

      3.

      4.

III. Conclusion. Type: _____ (from dyadic list)

Interviewee Persuasive Message Strategy

Claim Statement: I want my interviewer to primarily *agree to highly recommend me for the next interview* as a result of our employment interview.

I. Introduction. Type:_____ (from dyadic list)

II. Body. Check this box: ☐ Inductive

Please note: Supporting points 1-4 under A-C (below) may be omitted.

   A. *Getting answers to questions about my qualifications*

      1.

      2.

      3.

      4.

   B. *Answering my questions*

      1.

      2.

      3.

      4.

   C. *Discussing areas of personal interest (spontaneous digressions/diversions)*

      1.

      2.

      3.

      4.

III. Conclusion. Type: _____ (from dyadic list)

☐ Check this box; your claim is *paraphrased* and *reinforced* here.

Chapter 14
Discovering Your Ethical Core

Just Like an Apple Core

The field of ethics is "the branch of philosophy, or type of science, that is concerned with a person's choices of right and wrong." And, ethical standards are "a person's reasons for these choices."

As a part of your personality, ethical standards resemble the core of an apple — invisible from the outside — yet central to everything that you think and do. In other words, ethical standards are the basis for every choice that you make regarding your speeches and your life.

Do you know what comprises your ethical standards — your *ethical core?* This chapter will help you answer this question which will result in a significant improvement in all aspects of your speech communication skills.

Which One Is Best?

Because the field of ethics is so large, for the sake of discussion, it is simplified here using *Occam's Razor*, or the "Principle of Parsimony," which states that the simplest explanation is the best explanation.

The result is the presentation of *three seminal ethical standards* — three fundamental or primary sets of ethical standards — that represent all your possible ethical choices. They are the *Kantian Ethical Standards* based on the philosophy of the eighteenth century German philosopher Immanuel Kant, the *Machiavellian Ethical Standards* based on the philosophy of Nicollo Machiavelli, the sixteenth century Italian philosopher, and the *Nietzschean Ethical Standards* based on the nineteenth century German philosopher Friedrich Nietzsche.

After considering the upcoming information, you can decide with confidence which one of these ethical standards is best. Based upon your choice at the end of the chapter, you will discover your ethical core.

Taking a Closer Look

The terms *means* and *ends* are frequently used in regard to the ethical standards. The graphics below explain the definition of each word. These definitions are followed by a side-by-side comparison of the three standards and quotes related to the subject of business.

Ends are the *goals* of one's ethical choices

Means are the *ways* of attaining one's goals

Kantian Ethical Standards	Machiavellian Ethical Standards	Nietzschean Ethical Standards
1. The means and ends are valued the same, or equally.	The ends are valued more than the means. The ends justify (show sufficient reasons for) the means, or the reverse.	The means and ends are not valued in any way.
2. Adhere to the philosophy of "win-win" with all sources and receivers to win.	Adhere to the philosophy of "win-lose" with some sources to win and some receivers to lose, or the reverse.	Adhere to the philosophy of "lose-lose" with all sources and receivers to lose.
3. Sources and receivers choose the same means and same ends.	Sources and receivers choose different means or different ends, or both.	Sources and receivers do not choose any means or any ends.
4. Sources and receivers communicate for their mutual benefit.	Sources and receivers communicate for their own benefit.	Sources and receivers do not communicate with each other.
5. Sources and receivers *always* consider each other as an end in themselves, *never* as a means to an end.	Sources and receivers consider each other as a means to a more highly valued end, or the reverse. They may *sometimes act* according to the Kantian or Nietzschean Ethical Standards as a means to their end, or the reverse.	Sources and receivers *never* consider each other as a means or ends.
6. Sources and receivers share information that is equally interesting to each other. This is called *being influential*.	Sources and receivers use rewards and punishments to communicate information. Rewards are more interesting than punishments, or the reverse. This is called *using influence*.	Sources and receivers *neither are influential nor use influence*. They have a conscious desire for the total destruction of themselves and others — a *will to power*.
7. Mass communication is a greatly enlarged process of equally benefiting all sources and receivers.	Mass communication is a greatly enlarged process of benefiting some sources more than some receivers, or the reverse.	Mass communication does not exist; however, mass destruction of all sources and receivers may occur randomly.
8. All sources and receivers agree to follow the same law. This type of law is called *Universal Law*.	Sources govern receivers, or the reverse, and follow law which is created by a government. More than one government exists. This type of law is called *Legalistic Law*.	All sources and receivers do not follow any law, and no government exists. This status is called *Anarchy*.

**KANT ON
BUSINESS ETHICS**

*"*No conflict exists objectively, in theory, between ethics [morals] and business [politics]. It only exists subjectively — in the selfish disposition of people. Such a conflict may remain since it serves as a whetstone (sharpening tool) for developing a person's virtue.*"*

*"*A person who wants to act virtuously in every way necessarily comes to grief among so many who are not virtuous. Therefore, if a person [prince] wants to be successful in business [maintain his rule], that person must learn how not to be virtuous and to use or not use this skill according to her needs.*"*

**MACHIAVELLI ON
BUSINESS ETHICS**

**NIETZSCHE ON
BUSINESS ETHICS**

*"*Everything (in business) deserves to perish; but one actually puts one's shoulder to the plough; one should choose to destroy (her business and the business of others).*"*

For more information, read Kant's *Metaphysical Foundations of Morals*, Machiavelli's *The Prince*, and Nietzsche's *Will to Power*. These are the primary sources for the explanation of each philosopher's standards.

The Big Issues

How do the three ethical standards relate to the major contemporary issues of our society? Here is a comparison of each standard to three such big issues; the first issue is *war*.

How do the Kantian Ethical Standards apply to war?

Kantian Standards state that people communicate for their mutual benefit; the killing of one person by another in war results in a loss of benefits, namely life, to the person who was killed. This is the first obvious violation of these standards.

And, since the loss of life in war is a "lose" type of situation and not a "win" type, it also is a violation of the Kantian "win-win" Standard.

Moreover, when one human being willingly kills another in war, the person who was killed was a means to the other person's end. So, this too is a violation of the Kantian Standard of always treating a person as an end in themselves.

Could there ever be a goal or end valued so highly that the killing involved in war could be justified? The Kantian Standards give a definitive answer to this question, for they specifically say that people *never* treat each other as a means to an end. Therefore, using the Kantian Ethical Standards, war is never morally right.

How do the Machiavellian Ethical Standards deal with the issue of war?

Machiavelli never states that killing a human being is a good thing, and he does not promote homicide as a goal. However, Machiavelli definitely allows the act of homicide as a *means*.

In the Machiavellian Standards, if there is an end that can provide a good enough reason, then the means, which include the killing of other human beings, can be justified as morally right. In other words, if the goal or end of a war is valued highly enough, perhaps by being an ideal such as freedom, then the means, the killing of other human beings in that war, are morally right. So, using the Machiavellian Ethical Standards, with the right ends, war is a morally correct action.

As for the Nietzschean Ethical Standards, because the means and ends are not valued at all, the presence of a goal or reason for war is never present. However, this does not mean that Nietzscheans do not want war; they do. Indeed, Nietzscheans *always want war*. Why? Because war perfectly satisfies their singular, absolute want — their conscious desire for the total annihilation of themselves and others. Therefore, using the Nietzschean Standards, war is always morally right.

Issue Number Two

Here is another major issue to consider using the three ethical standards: *abortion*.

Using the Kantian Ethical Standards, the end, a mother's freedom to choose what happens to her body during pregnancy, is a valued goal. However, are the means, the termination of her pregnancy or abortion, morally right?

Since abortion has been legalized in the United States, much has been learned about what it is. And, the prevailing view is that for most mothers, abortion is a painful, depressing, and traumatic experience. By using the first Kantian Standard, the issue of abortion can be clarified as whether or not these negative personal experiences, the means, are equal in value to the desired end — the freedom to choose or not choose to have an abortion.

Because pain, depression, and trauma are kinds of harms, or things not valued or desired, then when applying this initial Kantian Ethical Standard, the means and ends are not valued equally, and, therefore, abortion is morally wrong. Other Kantian Standards also concur with this perspective, as you will see when the positions of the other two standards are presented.

Now let us use the Machiavellian Ethical Standards to understand abortion. With these standards, if Legalistic Law is created that allows a mother to choose an abortion, then her subsequent choice of an abortion is morally right. However, when Legalistic Law is created that prohibits abortion, then this same choice is morally wrong. In other words, when using Machiavellian Standards, the government may determine whether abortion is morally right or wrong.

An important point to note is that Machiavellian Legalistic Law may or may not coincide with the Universal Law of the Kantian Standards. In other words, what is *legal* for Machiavellians may not necessarily be *moral* for Kantians. In regard to the abortion issue, the Machiavellian Legalistic Law that allows abortion does not coincide with Kantian Universal Law.

Several other Machiavellian Standards also support the choice of abortion as being morally right. An end such as freedom of choice, when a society values it highly, provides a sufficient reason or justification for the means, the abortion — even if killing is involved (just like in war). The mother also can make choices only for her benefit, and using "win-lose" terminology, she can choose to be the winner and the fetus to be the loser.

As for the Nietzschean Ethical Standards, as a legal issue, abortion simply does not exist.

An anarchy is present when applying these standards, so no laws are created or adhered to that either allow or deny abortion. Nonetheless, this status does not exclude or eliminate a person's actions. A person still has the conscious

desire to destroy herself and others. So, the morally right action when applying the Nietzschean Standards is to have an abortion.

The Ultimate Scenario

What about the ultimate scenario in which there is the choice of saving the life of the mother *or* the life of the fetus?

This choice may be the most difficult one regarding abortion, for it is the question of who should live and who should die — when both cannot survive. In regard to the ethical standards, this may be stated as the question of whether the end, preserving the mother's life, would make the means, the abortion with subsequent loss of the unborn child's life, a morally right choice.

In this situation, when applying the Machiavellian Standards, the choice of an abortion is morally right. And, the primary supporting standard is the same one as previously mentioned: The end justifies, or gives sufficient reasons for, the means — saving the life of the mother (the end) is a sufficient reason to terminate the life of the fetus (the means).

As you might imagine, the Kantian Standards still consider abortion as a morally wrong choice, even if it results in saving the life of the mother. For Kantians, the predicament of killing the mother or fetus is seen as what the ancient Greek philosopher Plato succinctly called the *choice of the lesser of two evils*.

In other words, the goal of saving *either* life (either one becoming the valued end) would not change the Kantian view that *both* of the only two possible means are morally wrong: the choice to kill the mother (when she is the mean) *and* the choice to kill the fetus (when it is the mean). This scenario also vividly illustrates that a "justifiable homicide," or killing of a person which is deemed to be morally right, does not exist when applying the Kantian Ethical Standards.

As for the Nietzschean Ethical Standards, the morally right action is to not save the life of the mother or the life of the fetus. Indeed, these standards are fulfilled when both die. This also demonstrates the Nietzschean Standard of "lose-lose" because no one benefits — both the mother and fetus lose their lives. As for prosecution of anyone for these losses, because no laws are in place, no one is apprehended or punished.

Justifiable Homicide

Let us return to the concept of justifiable homicide. Although a justifiable homicide is not part of the Kantian Standards, it does exist when applying the other two ethical standards.

Here is an example. A police sharpshooter is faced with the choice of allowing a hostage taker to kill additional hostages or to kill the hostage taker. In this scenario, in order to prevent more innocent people from dying, the police officer kills the hostage taker. Is this a justifiable homicide?

Using the Machiavellian Ethical Standards, it certainly is. Why? Because a legal system may decide that the ends, saving the lives of the hostages, provide good enough reasons for the means, the killing of the hostage taker. In other words, by applying the Machiavellian Standards, the homicide committed by the police officer may be considered morally right when the reasons are great enough according to a society's legal system.

Could this life-and-death situation ever be a reasonable exception to the Kantian Ethical Standards?

Kantian Standards are absolute standards and are based on Universal Law, a kind of law that all people follow under all circumstances, whereas Machiavellian Standards are relative standards that are based on the legality of a situation. Therefore, Kantian Standards *always*, without exception, consider the killing of the hostage taker as being morally wrong. In other words, when using Kantian Ethical Standards, *homicide* — the killing of one person by another — is always considered the same as *murder* — the unlawful and morally wrong act of killing a human being.

How about the Nietzschean Ethical Standards, how do they relate to this scenario and the concept of justifiable homicide?

No laws exist within the Nietzschean Standards, so any form of homicide may occur. As for the specific justification for homicide, the only motivation is this: the conscious desire to destroy oneself and others. By applying this Nietzschean Standard, the action of a police officer to kill a hostage taker, or anyone for that matter, is morally right — a justifiable homicide. Moreover, when this same Nietzschean Ethical

Standard is applied *to all other homicides as well as suicides,* they also are considered to be a form of justifiable homicide.

Issue Number Three

The last major contemporary issue that we will be looking at is *capital punishment.*

In light of the Kantian Ethical Standards and their perspective on the previous two issues, it should be obvious that a highly desired end, even the serving of justice, does not provide a sufficient reason to change the morally wrong act used as a means of achieving it: the killing of another human being. Therefore, the Kantian Standards always consider capital punishment as being morally wrong.

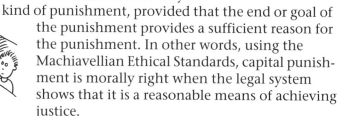

As for the Machiavellian Standards, the death penalty is an entirely different moral matter. These standards include the choice to use rewards and punishments. When a society chooses to change the criminal behavior of its members, Machiavellian Standards allow any

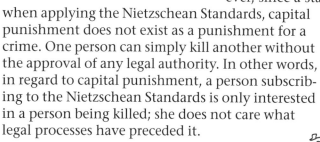

kind of punishment, provided that the end or goal of the punishment provides a sufficient reason for the punishment. In other words, using the Machiavellian Ethical Standards, capital punishment is morally right when the legal system shows that it is a reasonable means of achieving justice.

As for the Nietzschean Ethical Standards, because capital punishment is a way of destroying a person, it is wholeheartedly desired. However, since a state of anarchy or lawlessness exists

when applying the Nietzschean Standards, capital punishment does not exist as a punishment for a crime. One person can simply kill another without the approval of any legal authority. In other words, in regard to capital punishment, a person subscribing to the Nietzschean Standards is only interested in a person being killed; she does not care what legal processes have preceded it.

Do Not Be Fooled

Here is another key point: *A person subscribing to one of the three ethical standards as her ethical core may exhibit one or more personality traits of the other standards when making choices regarding these and other social issues.*

For example, a Machiavellian donates a large sum of money to charity. This appears to be a Kantian behavior, but is it? The answer is no. In this case, as a Machiavellian, she is treating the charity as if it were a valued end — a personality trait of a person who has a Kantian ethical core. For this Machiavellian, the donation

was actually a *means to her more highly valued end,* such as having her name published in the newspaper, getting a special award, receiving public recognition, or getting a tax benefit.

Here is another example. A person with a Nietzschean core practices a religion that believes in heaven, a goal or end for which to live one's life — a personality trait of a person subscribing to the Machiavellian or Kantian Standards. Is this person really a Nietzschean? As long as her ethical core is composed of the Nietzschean Ethical Standards, then the answer is yes, even though practicing a religion is an ethical choice that belongs to one of the other ethical standards.

Here is a final example regarding a person with a Kantian ethical core. A saleswoman does not like the product that she sells but needs the money from the job to support her family. In this case, although she possesses a Kantian ethical core, her job is a means to an end — she is behaving like a Machiavellian. So just like the previous examples, a personality trait of one ethical standard is being demonstrated while the same person contains a different ethical core.

Personal Issues

How do the three ethical standards relate to your personal, day-to-day issues? Here are five real-life scenarios to help you find out.

Answer each of the following questions *as if* you are a Kantian, then *as if* you are a Machiavellian, and finally *as if* you are a Nietzschean. Include the numbers of the standards that you used to make your choices.

Q. You are planning on selling your art as part of an upcoming speech assignment. Your room and board are paid by your parents; however, you could sell more art if you state that you need money for this month's rent. *Will you say this?*

Q. You want to miss a day of work to drive home to celebrate a close relative's birthday. You know that your supervisor will not approve your request since this is the busiest time of the year. *Will you give a more serious reason?*

Q. You are writing your resume for a particular job opening. The position requires two years' work experience, but you have only sixteen months' experience. *Will you leave out the exact months so that it appears that you have the required two years' experience?*

Q. You are close to graduating from college. You owe more than $50,000 in student loans and have more than $20,000 in credit-card debt. To rid yourself of financial stress, you could declare personal bankruptcy. *Will you?*

Q. A large tobacco company is about to hire you at a starting salary of $75,000 with a generous benefit package. You recently lost a close family member to lung cancer caused by smoking. *Will you accept the position?*

The Happiness Factor

And finally, an excellent way to learn about the ethical standards is by comparing them to a significant experience which they all have in common. One such experience is *happiness.*

"Which ethical standard is the *best* way to achieve happiness — the Kantian, Machiavellian, or Nietzschean?"

This is the key question to ask yourself as you read the following quotes from highly credible sources about happiness.

Happiness is the meaning and the purpose of life,
the whole aim and end of human existence.

Aristotle

Be in general virtuous and you will be happy.

Ben Franklin

A person who achieves wealth and power by excluding justice and
virtue will lose the health of her body. Life, in this case, is no longer
endurable, although pampered with all kinds of meats and drinks. Is
such a life worth living? The question itself is ridiculous.

Plato

The supreme happiness in life is the conviction
that we are loved.

Victor Hugo

The person is happiest, whether rich or poor,
who finds peace in their home.

Johann von Goethe

*Most people are about as happy as they make up
their minds to be.*

Abraham Lincoln

*Seek to do good and you will find that happiness
will run after you.*

James Freeman Clarke

*The care of human life and happiness, and not their destruction, is the
first and only legitimate object of good government.*

Thomas Jefferson

A joy that is shared is a joy made double.

English Proverb

So What Is Your Choice?

It is now time to discover your ethical core.

You can make this discovery by choosing one of the three ethical standards presented in this chapter. And, because your happiness depends on this decision, you need to choose carefully.

So, which set of standards do you think is best?

Kantian Ethical Standards

Machiavellian Ethical Standards

Nietzschean Ethical Standards

Appendix

Blank Communication Guides (Six)
Interview Persuasive Message Strategies (Six)
Discussion Formats (Six)
(perforated)

Communication Guide

Claim Statement (Step 1)

In terms of your receivers' knowledge, attitudes, and behaviors, what is your *single* most-desired change? Write this desired change as your claim through use of this format:

I want my receivers to primarily *know, believe,* or *do* (circle one)

_____

_____ as a result of listening to my speech.

Receiver Analysis (Step 2)

Analyze your receivers through use of the following criteria.

1. *Demographics*: In terms of your claim, how would you describe your receivers as a group?

Cultural/Physical (external traits)	*Psychological* (internal traits)
a.	a.
b.	b.
c.	c.
d.	d.
e.	e.

2. *Knowledge:* In terms of your claim, what kinds of facts or factual levels — in any order — are your receivers highly interested in? (Cue words: *knowing who, what, when, where, why, or how . . .*)

a.

b.

c.

d.

e.

3. *Attitudes:* In terms of your claim, what kinds of opinions are your receivers highly interested in? (Cue words: *believing/believing that . . .*)

    a.

    b.

    c.

    d.

    e.

4. *Behaviors:* In terms of your claim, what kinds of experiences are your receivers highly interested in? (Cue word: *experiencing an "-ing" word at the start of each answer below*)

    a.

    b.

    c.

    d.

    e.

Source Credibility Analysis (Step 3)

Analyze your source credibility through use of the following criteria.

Communicating source credibility: Using your Receiver Analysis, how do you plan to communicate high source credibility? Namely, by: *citing credentials, citing experience, citing other highly credible people, citing yourself, and citing demographics*? Please explain.

    a. Could quote/state/relate . . .

    b. Could quote/state/relate . . .

    c. Could quote/state/relate . . .

    d. Could quote/state/relate . . .

    e. Could quote/state/relate . . .

Channel Characteristics Analysis (Step 4)

Analyze your communication channels through use of the following criteria.

Channel utilization: Using your Receiver Analysis, what interesting communication channels, namely: *kinesics, haptics, visual/sensory aids, paralinguistics, chronemics, proxemics, dress, and monosensory aids* do you plan to use? Please explain.

a. Could show/give/wear . . .

b. Could show/give/wear . . .

c. Could show/give/wear . . .

d. Could show/give/wear . . .

e. Could show/give/wear . . .

Persuasive Message Strategy (Step 5)

Claim Statement: I want my receivers to primarily *know, believe,* or *do* (circle one)

_____

_____ as a result of listening to my speech.

I. Introduction. Type: _____

☐ Check this box if your claim is paraphrased and reinforced here, *or* check the box located in the conclusion.

II. Body. Check one: ☐ Inductive ☐ Deductive

The body includes at least three major points, A-C, with at least four supporting points. A-C also are kinds of behavioral-level information from your Receiver Analysis that start with "*-ing*" words such as *learning, feeling, enjoying, eating, viewing,* or other similar words.

A.

   1.

   2.

   3.

   4.

B.

   1.

   2.

   3.

   4.

C.

   1.

   2.

   3.

   4.

III. Conclusion. Type: _____

☐ Check this box if your claim is paraphrased and reinforced here.

Communication Guide

Claim Statement (Step 1)

In terms of your receivers' knowledge, attitudes, and behaviors, what is your *single* most-desired change? Write this desired change as your claim through use of this format:

I want my receivers to primarily *know, believe,* or *do* (circle one)

_____

_____ as a result of listening to my speech.

Receiver Analysis (Step 2)

Analyze your receivers through use of the following criteria.

1. *Demographics*: In terms of your claim, how would you describe your receivers as a group?

Cultural/Physical (external traits)	*Psychological* (internal traits)
a.	a.
b.	b.
c.	c.
d.	d.
e.	e.

2. *Knowledge:* In terms of your claim, what kinds of facts or factual levels — in any order — are your receivers highly interested in? (Cue words: *knowing who, what, when, where, why, or how . . .*)

a.

b.

c.

d.

e.

3. *Attitudes:* In terms of your claim, what kinds of opinions are your receivers highly interested in? (Cue words: *believing/believing that . . .*)

a.

b.

c.

d.

e.

4. *Behaviors:* In terms of your claim, what kinds of experiences are your receivers highly interested in? (Cue word: *experiencing an "-ing" word at the start of each answer below*)

a.

b.

c.

d.

e.

Source Credibility Analysis (Step 3)

Analyze your source credibility through use of the following criteria.

Communicating source credibility: Using your Receiver Analysis, how do you plan to communicate high source credibility? Namely, by: *citing credentials, citing experience, citing other highly credible people, citing yourself, and citing demographics*? Please explain.

a. Could quote/state/relate . . .

b. Could quote/state/relate . . .

c. Could quote/state/relate . . .

d. Could quote/state/relate . . .

e. Could quote/state/relate . . .

Channel Characteristics Analysis (Step 4)

Analyze your communication channels through use of the following criteria.

Channel utilization: Using your Receiver Analysis, what interesting communication channels, namely: *kinesics, haptics, visual/sensory aids, paralinguistics, chronemics, proxemics, dress, and monosensory aids* do you plan to use? Please explain.

a. Could show/give/wear . . .

b. Could show/give/wear . . .

c. Could show/give/wear . . .

d. Could show/give/wear . . .

e. Could show/give/wear . . .

Persuasive Message Strategy (Step 5)

Claim Statement: I want my receivers to primarily *know, believe,* or *do* (circle one)

_____

_____ as a result of listening to my speech.

I. Introduction. Type: _____

☐ Check this box if your claim is paraphrased and reinforced here, *or* check the box located in the conclusion.

II. Body. Check one: ☐ Inductive ☐ Deductive

The body includes at least three major points, A-C, with at least four supporting points. A-C also are kinds of behavioral-level information from your Receiver Analysis that start with "*-ing*" words such as *learning, feeling, enjoying, eating, viewing,* or other similar words.

   A.

      1.

      2.

      3.

      4.

   B.

      1.

      2.

      3.

      4.

   C.

      1.

      2.

      3.

      4.

III. Conclusion. Type: _____

☐ Check this box if your claim is paraphrased and reinforced here.

Communication Guide

Claim Statement (Step 1)

In terms of your receivers' knowledge, attitudes, and behaviors, what is your *single* most-desired change? Write this desired change as your claim through use of this format:

I want my receivers to primarily *know, believe,* or *do* (circle one)

_____

_____ as a result of listening to my speech.

Receiver Analysis (Step 2)

Analyze your receivers through use of the following criteria.

1. *Demographics*: In terms of your claim, how would you describe your receivers as a group?

Cultural/Physical (external traits)	*Psychological* (internal traits)
a.	a.
b.	b.
c.	c.
d.	d.
e.	e.

2. *Knowledge:* In terms of your claim, what kinds of facts or factual levels — in any order — are your receivers highly interested in? (Cue words: *knowing who, what, when, where, why, or how . . .*)

a.

b.

c.

d.

e.

3. *Attitudes:* In terms of your claim, what kinds of opinions are your receivers highly interested in? (Cue words: *believing/believing that . . .*)

a.

b.

c.

d.

e.

4. *Behaviors:* In terms of your claim, what kinds of experiences are your receivers highly interested in? (Cue word: *experiencing an "-ing" word at the start of each answer below*)

a.

b.

c.

d.

e.

Source Credibility Analysis (Step 3)

Analyze your source credibility through use of the following criteria.

Communicating source credibility: Using your Receiver Analysis, how do you plan to communicate high source credibility? Namely, by: *citing credentials, citing experience, citing other highly credible people, citing yourself, and citing demographics?* Please explain.

a. Could quote/state/relate . . .

b. Could quote/state/relate . . .

c. Could quote/state/relate . . .

d. Could quote/state/relate . . .

e. Could quote/state/relate . . .

Channel Characteristics Analysis (Step 4)

Analyze your communication channels through use of the following criteria.

Channel utilization: Using your Receiver Analysis, what interesting communication channels, namely: *kinesics, haptics, visual/sensory aids, paralinguistics, chronemics, proxemics, dress, and monosensory aids* do you plan to use? Please explain.

a. Could show/give/wear . . .

b. Could show/give/wear . . .

c. Could show/give/wear . . .

d. Could show/give/wear . . .

e. Could show/give/wear . . .

Persuasive Message Strategy (Step 5)

Claim Statement: I want my receivers to primarily *know, believe,* or *do* (circle one)

_____

_____ as a result of listening to my speech.

I. Introduction. Type: _____

☐ Check this box if your claim is paraphrased and reinforced here, *or* check the box located in the conclusion.

II. Body. Check one: ☐ Inductive ☐ Deductive

The body includes at least three major points, A-C, with at least four supporting points. A-C also are kinds of behavioral-level information from your Receiver Analysis that start with "*-ing*" words such as *learning, feeling, enjoying, eating, viewing,* or other similar words.

A.

    1.

    2.

    3.

    4.

B.

    1.

    2.

    3.

    4.

C.

    1.

    2.

    3.

    4.

III. Conclusion. Type: _____

☐ Check this box if your claim is paraphrased and reinforced here.

Communication Guide

Claim Statement (Step 1)

In terms of your receivers' knowledge, attitudes, and behaviors, what is your *single* most-desired change? Write this desired change as your claim through use of this format:

I want my receivers to primarily *know, believe,* or *do* (circle one)

_____

_____ as a result of listening to my speech.

Receiver Analysis (Step 2)

Analyze your receivers through use of the following criteria.

1. *Demographics*: In terms of your claim, how would you describe your receivers as a group?

Cultural/Physical (external traits)	*Psychological* (internal traits)
a.	a.
b.	b.
c.	c.
d.	d.
e.	e.

2. *Knowledge:* In terms of your claim, what kinds of facts or factual levels — in any order — are your receivers highly interested in? (Cue words: *knowing who, what, when, where, why, or how . . .*)

a.

b.

c.

d.

e.

3. *Attitudes:* In terms of your claim, what kinds of opinions are your receivers highly interested in? (Cue words: *believing/believing that . . .*)

a.

b.

c.

d.

e.

4. *Behaviors:* In terms of your claim, what kinds of experiences are your receivers highly interested in? (Cue word: *experiencing an "-ing" word at the start of each answer below*)

a.

b.

c.

d.

e.

Source Credibility Analysis (Step 3)

Analyze your source credibility through use of the following criteria.

Communicating source credibility: Using your Receiver Analysis, how do you plan to communicate high source credibility? Namely, by: *citing credentials, citing experience, citing other highly credible people, citing yourself, and citing demographics?* Please explain.

a. Could quote/state/relate . . .

b. Could quote/state/relate . . .

c. Could quote/state/relate . . .

d. Could quote/state/relate . . .

e. Could quote/state/relate . . .

Channel Characteristics Analysis (Step 4)

Analyze your communication channels through use of the following criteria.

Channel utilization: Using your Receiver Analysis, what interesting communication channels, namely: *kinesics, haptics, visual/sensory aids, paralinguistics, chronemics, proxemics, dress, and monosensory aids* do you plan to use? Please explain.

a. Could show/give/wear . . .

b. Could show/give/wear . . .

c. Could show/give/wear . . .

d. Could show/give/wear . . .

e. Could show/give/wear . . .

Persuasive Message Strategy (Step 5)

Claim Statement: I want my receivers to primarily *know, believe,* or *do* (circle one)

_____

_____ as a result of listening to my speech.

I. Introduction. Type: _____

☐ Check this box if your claim is paraphrased and reinforced here, *or* check the box located in the conclusion.

II. Body. Check one: ☐ Inductive ☐ Deductive

The body includes at least three major points, A-C, with at least four supporting points. A-C also are kinds of behavioral-level information from your Receiver Analysis that start with "*-ing*" words such as *learning, feeling, enjoying, eating, viewing,* or other similar words.

A.

   1.

   2.

   3.

   4.

B.

   1.

   2.

   3.

   4.

C.

   1.

   2.

   3.

   4.

III. Conclusion. Type: _____

☐ Check this box if your claim is paraphrased and reinforced here.

Communication Guide

Claim Statement (Step 1)

In terms of your receivers' knowledge, attitudes, and behaviors, what is your *single* most-desired change? Write this desired change as your claim through use of this format:

I want my receivers to primarily *know, believe,* or *do* (circle one)

_____

_____ as a result of listening to my speech.

Receiver Analysis (Step 2)

Analyze your receivers through use of the following criteria.

1. *Demographics*: In terms of your claim, how would you describe your receivers as a group?

Cultural/Physical (external traits)	*Psychological* (internal traits)
a.	a.
b.	b.
c.	c.
d.	d.
e.	e.

2. *Knowledge:* In terms of your claim, what kinds of facts or factual levels — in any order — are your receivers highly interested in? (Cue words: *knowing who, what, when, where, why, or how . . .*)

a.

b.

c.

d.

e.

3. *Attitudes:* In terms of your claim, what kinds of opinions are your receivers highly interested in? (Cue words: *believing/believing that . . .*)

    a.

    b.

    c.

    d.

    e.

4. *Behaviors:* In terms of your claim, what kinds of experiences are your receivers highly interested in? (Cue word: *experiencing an "-ing" word at the start of each answer below*)

    a.

    b.

    c.

    d.

    e.

Source Credibility Analysis (Step 3)

Analyze your source credibility through use of the following criteria.

Communicating source credibility: Using your Receiver Analysis, how do you plan to communicate high source credibility? Namely, by: *citing credentials, citing experience, citing other highly credible people, citing yourself, and citing demographics*? Please explain.

    a. Could quote/state/relate . . .

    b. Could quote/state/relate . . .

    c. Could quote/state/relate . . .

    d. Could quote/state/relate . . .

    e. Could quote/state/relate . . .

Channel Characteristics Analysis (Step 4)

Analyze your communication channels through use of the following criteria.

Channel utilization: Using your Receiver Analysis, what interesting communication channels, namely: *kinesics, haptics, visual/sensory aids, paralinguistics, chronemics, proxemics, dress, and monosensory aids* do you plan to use? Please explain.

a. Could show/give/wear . . .

b. Could show/give/wear . . .

c. Could show/give/wear . . .

d. Could show/give/wear . . .

e. Could show/give/wear . . .

Persuasive Message Strategy (Step 5)

Claim Statement: I want my receivers to primarily *know, believe,* or *do* (circle one)

_____

_____ as a result of listening to my speech.

I. Introduction. Type: _____

☐ Check this box if your claim is paraphrased and reinforced here, *or* check the box located in the conclusion.

II. Body. Check one: ☐ Inductive ☐ Deductive

The body includes at least three major points, A-C, with at least four supporting points. A-C also are kinds of behavioral-level information from your Receiver Analysis that start with "*-ing*" words such as *learning, feeling, enjoying, eating, viewing,* or other similar words.

   A.

      1.

      2.

      3.

      4.

   B.

      1.

      2.

      3.

      4.

   C.

      1.

      2.

      3.

      4.

III. Conclusion. Type: _____

☐ Check this box if your claim is paraphrased and reinforced here.

Communication Guide

Claim Statement (Step 1)

In terms of your receivers' knowledge, attitudes, and behaviors, what is your *single* most-desired change? Write this desired change as your claim through use of this format:

I want my receivers to primarily *know, believe,* or *do* (circle one)

_____

_____ as a result of listening to my speech.

Receiver Analysis (Step 2)

Analyze your receivers through use of the following criteria.

1. *Demographics*: In terms of your claim, how would you describe your receivers as a group?

Cultural/Physical (external traits)	*Psychological* (internal traits)
a.	a.
b.	b.
c.	c.
d.	d.
e.	e.

2. *Knowledge:* In terms of your claim, what kinds of facts or factual levels — in any order — are your receivers highly interested in? (Cue words: *knowing who, what, when, where, why, or how . . .*)

a.

b.

c.

d.

e.

3. *Attitudes:* In terms of your claim, what kinds of opinions are your receivers highly interested in? (Cue words: *believing/believing that . . .*)

    a.

    b.

    c.

    d.

    e.

4. *Behaviors:* In terms of your claim, what kinds of experiences are your receivers highly interested in? (Cue word: *experiencing an "-ing" word at the start of each answer below*)

    a.

    b.

    c.

    d.

    e.

Source Credibility Analysis (Step 3)

Analyze your source credibility through use of the following criteria.

Communicating source credibility: Using your Receiver Analysis, how do you plan to communicate high source credibility? Namely, by: *citing credentials, citing experience, citing other highly credible people, citing yourself, and citing demographics*? Please explain.

    a. Could quote/state/relate . . .

    b. Could quote/state/relate . . .

    c. Could quote/state/relate . . .

    d. Could quote/state/relate . . .

    e. Could quote/state/relate . . .

Channel Characteristics Analysis (Step 4)

Analyze your communication channels through use of the following criteria.

Channel utilization: Using your Receiver Analysis, what interesting communication channels, namely: *kinesics, haptics, visual/sensory aids, paralinguistics, chronemics, proxemics, dress, and monosensory aids* do you plan to use? Please explain.

a. Could show/give/wear . . .

b. Could show/give/wear . . .

c. Could show/give/wear . . .

d. Could show/give/wear . . .

e. Could show/give/wear . . .

Persuasive Message Strategy (Step 5)

Claim Statement: I want my receivers to primarily *know, believe,* or *do* (circle one)

_____

_____ as a result of listening to my speech.

I. Introduction. Type: _____

☐ Check this box if your claim is paraphrased and reinforced here, *or* check the box located in the conclusion.

II. Body. Check one: ☐ Inductive ☐ Deductive

The body includes at least three major points, A-C, with at least four supporting points. A-C also are kinds of behavioral-level information from your Receiver Analysis that start with "*-ing*" words such as *learning, feeling, enjoying, eating, viewing,* or other similar words.

  A.

    1.

    2.

    3.

    4.

  B.

    1.

    2.

    3.

    4.

  C.

    1.

    2.

    3.

    4.

III. Conclusion. Type: _____

☐ Check this box if your claim is paraphrased and reinforced here.

Interviewer Persuasive Message Strategy

Claim Statement: I want my interviewee to primarily *agree to prove that she is the most qualified applicant* as a result of our employment interview.

I. Introduction. Type:_____ (from dyadic list)

☐ Check this box; your claim is *paraphrased* and *reinforced* here.

II. Body. Check this box: ☐ Deductive

Please note: Supporting points 1-4 under A-D (below) may be omitted.

   A. *Learning about the job and company*

      1.

      2.

      3.

      4.

   B. *Being asked questions about qualifications*

      1.

      2.

      3.

      4.

   C. *Asking me questions*

      1.

      2.

      3.

      4.

   D. *Discussing areas of personal interest (spontaneous digressions/diversions)*

      1.

      2.

      3.

      4.

III. Conclusion. Type: _____ (from dyadic list)

Interviewer Persuasive Message Strategy

Claim Statement: I want my interviewee to primarily *agree to prove that she is the most qualified applicant* as a result of our employment interview.

I. Introduction. Type:_____ (from dyadic list)

☐ Check this box; your claim is *paraphrased* and *reinforced* here.

II. Body. Check this box: ☐ Deductive

Please note: Supporting points 1-4 under A-D (below) may be omitted.

   A. *Learning about the job and company*

      1.

      2.

      3.

      4.

   B. *Being asked questions about qualifications*

      1.

      2.

      3.

      4.

   C. *Asking me questions*

      1.

      2.

      3.

      4.

   D. *Discussing areas of personal interest (spontaneous digressions/diversions)*

      1.

      2.

      3.

      4.

III. Conclusion. Type: _____ (from dyadic list)

Interviewer Persuasive Message Strategy

Claim Statement: I want my interviewee to primarily *agree to prove that she is the most qualified applicant* as a result of our employment interview.

I. Introduction. Type:_____ (from dyadic list)

☐ Check this box; your claim is *paraphrased* and *reinforced* here.

II. Body. Check this box: ☐ Deductive

Please note: Supporting points 1-4 under A-D (below) may be omitted.

   A. *Learning about the job and company*

      1.

      2.

      3.

      4.

   B. *Being asked questions about qualifications*

      1.

      2.

      3.

      4.

   C. *Asking me questions*

      1.

      2.

      3.

      4.

   D. *Discussing areas of personal interest (spontaneous digressions/diversions)*

      1.

      2.

      3.

      4.

III. Conclusion. Type: _____ (from dyadic list)

Interviewer Persuasive Message Strategy

Claim Statement: I want my interviewee to primarily *agree to prove that she is the most qualified applicant* as a result of our employment interview.

I. Introduction. Type:_____ (from dyadic list)

☐ Check this box; your claim is *paraphrased* and *reinforced* here.

II. Body. Check this box: ☐ Deductive

Please note: Supporting points 1-4 under A-D (below) may be omitted.

   A. *Learning about the job and company*

      1.

      2.

      3.

      4.

   B. *Being asked questions about qualifications*

      1.

      2.

      3.

      4.

   C. *Asking me questions*

      1.

      2.

      3.

      4.

   D. *Discussing areas of personal interest (spontaneous digressions/diversions)*

      1.

      2.

      3.

      4.

III. Conclusion. Type: _____ (from dyadic list)

Interviewer Persuasive Message Strategy

Claim Statement: I want my interviewee to primarily *agree to prove that she is the most qualified applicant* as a result of our employment interview.

I. Introduction. Type:_____ (from dyadic list)

☐ Check this box; your claim is *paraphrased* and *reinforced* here.

II. Body. Check this box: ☐ Deductive

Please note: Supporting points 1-4 under A-D (below) may be omitted.

   A. *Learning about the job and company*

      1.

      2.

      3.

      4.

   B. *Being asked questions about qualifications*

      1.

      2.

      3.

      4.

   C. *Asking me questions*

      1.

      2.

      3.

      4.

   D. *Discussing areas of personal interest (spontaneous digressions/diversions)*

      1.

      2.

      3.

      4.

III. Conclusion. Type: _____ (from dyadic list)

Interviewer Persuasive Message Strategy

Claim Statement: I want my interviewee to primarily *agree to prove that she is the most qualified applicant* as a result of our employment interview.

I. Introduction. Type:_____ (from dyadic list)

☐ Check this box; your claim is *paraphrased* and *reinforced* here.

II. Body. Check this box: ☐ Deductive

Please note: Supporting points 1-4 under A-D (below) may be omitted.

  A. *Learning about the job and company*

     1.

     2.

     3.

     4.

  B. *Being asked questions about qualifications*

     1.

     2.

     3.

     4.

  C. *Asking me questions*

     1.

     2.

     3.

     4.

  D. *Discussing areas of personal interest (spontaneous digressions/diversions)*

     1.

     2.

     3.

     4.

III. Conclusion. Type: _____ (from dyadic list)

Interviewee Persuasive Message Strategy

Claim Statement: I want my interviewer to primarily *agree to highly recommend me for the next interview* as a result of our employment interview.

I. Introduction. Type: _____ (from dyadic list)

II. Body. Check this box: ☐ Inductive

Please note: Supporting points 1-4 under A-C (below) may be omitted.

   A. *Getting answers to questions about my qualifications*

      1.

      2.

      3.

      4.

   B. *Answering my questions*

      1.

      2.

      3.

      4.

   C. *Discussing areas of personal interest (spontaneous digressions/diversions)*

      1.

      2.

      3.

      4.

III. Conclusion. Type: _____ (from dyadic list)

☐ Check this box; your claim is *paraphrased* and *reinforced* here.

Interviewee Persuasive Message Strategy

Claim Statement: I want my interviewer to primarily *agree to highly recommend me for the next interview* as a result of our employment interview.

I. Introduction. Type: _____ (from dyadic list)

II. Body. Check this box: ☐ Inductive

Please note: Supporting points 1-4 under A-C (below) may be omitted.

   A. *Getting answers to questions about my qualifications*

      1.

      2.

      3.

      4.

   B. *Answering my questions*

      1.

      2.

      3.

      4.

   C. *Discussing areas of personal interest (spontaneous digressions/diversions)*

      1.

      2.

      3.

      4.

III. Conclusion. Type: _____ (from dyadic list)

☐ Check this box; your claim is *paraphrased* and *reinforced* here.

Interviewee Persuasive Message Strategy

Claim Statement: I want my interviewer to primarily *agree to highly recommend me for the next interview* as a result of our employment interview.

I. Introduction. Type:_____ (from dyadic list)

II. Body. Check this box: ☐ Inductive

Please note: Supporting points 1-4 under A-C (below) may be omitted.

    A. *Getting answers to questions about my qualifications*

        1.

        2.

        3.

        4.

    B. *Answering my questions*

        1.

        2.

        3.

        4.

    C. *Discussing areas of personal interest (spontaneous digressions/diversions)*

        1.

        2.

        3.

        4.

III. Conclusion. Type: _____ (from dyadic list)

☐ Check this box; your claim is *paraphrased* and *reinforced* here.

Interviewee Persuasive Message Strategy

Claim Statement: I want my interviewer to primarily *agree to highly recommend me for the next interview* as a result of our employment interview.

I. Introduction. Type:_____ (from dyadic list)

II. Body. Check this box: ☐ Inductive

Please note: Supporting points 1-4 under A-C (below) may be omitted.

   A. *Getting answers to questions about my qualifications*

      1.

      2.

      3.

      4.

   B. *Answering my questions*

      1.

      2.

      3.

      4.

   C. *Discussing areas of personal interest (spontaneous digressions/diversions)*

      1.

      2.

      3.

      4.

III. Conclusion. Type. _____ (from dyadic list)

☐ Check this box; your claim is *paraphrased* and *reinforced* here.

Interviewee Persuasive Message Strategy

Claim Statement: I want my interviewer to primarily *agree to highly recommend me for the next interview* as a result of our employment interview.

I. Introduction. Type:_____ (from dyadic list)

II. Body. Check this box: ☐ Inductive

Please note: Supporting points 1-4 under A-C (below) may be omitted.

   A. *Getting answers to questions about my qualifications*

      1.

      2.

      3.

      4.

   B. *Answering my questions*

      1.

      2.

      3.

      4.

   C. *Discussing areas of personal interest (spontaneous digressions/diversions)*

      1.

      2.

      3.

      4.

III. Conclusion. Type: _____ (from dyadic list)

☐ Check this box; your claim is *paraphrased* and *reinforced* here.

Interviewee **Persuasive Message Strategy**

Claim Statement: I want my interviewer to primarily *agree to highly recommend me for the next interview* as a result of our employment interview.

I. Introduction. Type:_____ (from dyadic list)

II. Body. Check this box: ☐ Inductive

Please note: Supporting points 1-4 under A-C (below) may be omitted.

   A. *Getting answers to questions about my qualifications*

      1.

      2.

      3.

      4.

   B. *Answering my questions*

      1.

      2.

      3.

      4.

   C. *Discussing areas of personal interest (spontaneous digressions/diversions)*

      1.

      2.

      3.

      4.

III. Conclusion. Type: _____ (from dyadic list)

☐ Check this box; your claim is *paraphrased* and *reinforced* here.

Discussion Format

Start your discussion by saying:

First, could you please tell me what you think my claim is?

Then use the "compliment sandwich":

1. What is one thing about my speech that you liked?

2. In order to help me, could you please give me one suggestion regarding how I could improve my speech?

3. As before, what is another thing about my speech that you liked?

Conclude by saying:

And finally, do you have any other comments or questions regarding my speech?

After all responses, then say:

Thanks for your help!

Discussion Format

Start your discussion by saying:

First, could you please tell me what you think my claim is?

Then use the "compliment sandwich":

1. What is one thing about my speech that you liked?

2. In order to help me, could you please give me one suggestion regarding how I could improve my speech?

3. As before, what is another thing about my speech that you liked?

Conclude by saying:

And finally, do you have any other comments or questions regarding my speech?

After all responses, then say:

Thanks for your help!

Discussion Format

Start your discussion by saying:

First, could you please tell me what you think my claim is?

Then use the "compliment sandwich":

1. What is one thing about my speech that you liked?

2. In order to help me, could you please give me one suggestion regarding how I could improve my speech?

3. As before, what is another thing about my speech that you liked?

Conclude by saying:

And finally, do you have any other comments or questions regarding my speech?

After all responses, then say:

Thanks for your help!

Discussion Format

Start your discussion by saying:

First, could you please tell me what you think my claim is?

Then use the "compliment sandwich":

1. What is one thing about my speech that you liked?

2. In order to help me, could you please give me one suggestion regarding how I could improve my speech?

3. As before, what is another thing about my speech that you liked?

Conclude by saying:

And finally, do you have any other comments or questions regarding my speech?

After all responses, then say:

Thanks for your help!

Discussion Format

Start your discussion by saying:

First, could you please tell me what you think my claim is?

Then use the "compliment sandwich":

1. What is one thing about my speech that you liked?

2. In order to help me, could you please give me one suggestion regarding how I could improve my speech?

3. As before, what is another thing about my speech that you liked?

Conclude by saying:

And finally, do you have any other comments or questions regarding my speech?

After all responses, then say:

Thanks for your help!

Discussion Format

Start your discussion by saying:

First, could you please tell me what you think my claim is?

Then use the "compliment sandwich":

1. What is one thing about my speech that you liked?

2. In order to help me, could you please give me one suggestion regarding how I could improve my speech?

3. As before, what is another thing about my speech that you liked?

Conclude by saying:

And finally, do you have any other comments or questions regarding my speech?

After all responses, then say:

Thanks for your help!